CRIMINAL DEFENSE-BASED FORENSIC SOCIAL WORK

This book draws upon the Colorado Model of Criminal Defense-Based Forensic Social Work—a holistic, client-centered, collaborative approach that uses a trauma-informed care framework—to outline the numerous roles and skills of a forensic social worker. The comprehensive, developmentally informed model employs a *past* (e.g., mitigation themes and life history compilation), *present* (e.g., client contact and current functioning support), and *future* (e.g., reentry services) framework to provide mitigation narratives for defendants and to create a comprehensive approach to service.

The text starts with an overview of practice standards, ethical considerations, and legal frameworks. Next, chapters examine the unique roles that a forensic social worker must take on and the skills they need to possess. These include using clinical interventions with clients in nonclinical settings, working with clients of different identities and backgrounds, assisting with reentry planning for incarcerated clients, and collaborating with experts outside of the defense team. Finally, the authors provide strategies for practitioners to engage in their own self-care.

Interwoven with four case studies using the Colorado Model, this book will be valuable reading for graduate schools of social work, law school programs which have clinics or direct practice components to legal studies, and at defender agencies who contract with or employ social workers on staff.

Ashley Ratliff, JD, MSW, has been a juvenile defense attorney in Colorado for over 10 years. Ms. Ratliff is an expert in comprehensive, holistic child-centered litigation for youth prosecuted in adult and juvenile courts. She currently leads the Youth in Adult Court Litigation Committee for the Colorado Juvenile Defender Center (CJDC) and is an Adjunct Professor at the University of Denver's Graduate School of Social Work.

Maren Willins, LCSW, is a criminal defense-based forensic social worker and psychotherapist in the Denver metro area. She is a licensed clinical social worker and has been working in the public and private criminal justice field for over 15 years. Ms. Willins has also had her own psychotherapy private practice for over 10 years, in which she provides solution-focused and client-centered therapy for individuals as well as supervision to new social workers.

"*Criminal Defense-Based Forensic Social Work* describes social workers who appreciate the needs of clients and effectively tell their stories to achieve developmentally-sound justice. Their innovative approach as part of the defense team, the diverse social work talents required, and their skillful collaboration with families and others are demonstrated through four clients woven into the book's eight information-packed chapters. *Criminal Defense-Based Forensic Social Work* is inspiring for all of us working in juvenile and criminal court!"

Marty Beyer, PhD, juvenile justice and child welfare consultant

"After working over 25 years in forensic practice, it is great to have a book that examines the practice of defense-based forensic social work. The contributors have provided us with a great tool for enhancing our knowledge and teaching, while educating the criminal justice community. The book reveals the most critical aspects and duties required by social workers involved in criminal defense work."

Lori James-Townes, MSW-LCSW-C, Lecturer, Department of Family Studies & Community Development, Towson University

"This book provides valuable information about the variety of pertinent issues that a forensic social worker encounters. What is most helpful about the format of the book is the comprehensive yet concise manner in which a multitude of information is delivered. *Criminal Defense-Based Forensic Social Work* is an important contribution to the field of forensic social work. I highly recommend this book to any new or seasoned forensic social worker!"

Carol Heinisch, MA, LCSW, Colorado State Public Defenders Office

CRIMINAL DEFENSE-BASED FORENSIC SOCIAL WORK

Edited by Ashley Ratliff and Maren Willins

Routledge
Taylor & Francis Group
NEW YORK AND LONDON

First published 2019
by Routledge
711 Third Avenue, New York, NY 10017

and by Routledge
2 Park Square, Milton Park, Abingdon, Oxon, OX14 4RN

Routledge is an imprint of the Taylor & Francis Group, an informa business

Library of Congress Cataloging-in-Publication Data
Names: Ratliff, Ashley, editor. | Willins, Maren, editor.
Title: Criminal defense-based forensic social work /
edited by Ashley Ratliff and Maren Willins.
Description: 1 Edition. | New York: Routledge, 2019.
Identifiers: LCCN 2018026491 | ISBN 9781138221536
(hardcover: alk. paper) | ISBN 9781138221543 (pbk.) |
ISBN 9781315410173 (e-book)
Subjects: LCSH: Forensic psychology. |
Social service. | Evidence, Expert.
Classification: LCC RA1148 .C74 2019 | DDC 614/.15—dc23
LC record available at https://lccn.loc.gov/2018026491

ISBN: 978-1-138-22153-6 (hbk)
ISBN: 978-1-138-22154-3 (pbk)
ISBN: 978-1-315-41017-3 (ebk)

Typeset in Bembo
by codeMantra

CONTENTS

FOREWORD

Tina Maschi

Over 20 years ago, I began my social work career as a licensed clinical social worker in a prison hospital that served juveniles, adults, and older adults. I witnessed firsthand a justice system inadequately prepared to address a host of vulnerable groups with special needs, including youth, racial/ethnic minorities, older and lesbian, gay, bisexual, and transgender (LGBT) people, and persons with mental and physical disabilities. I also witnessed firsthand how social work education offered minimal support in providing the knowledge, values, and skills necessary to work with forensic populations, such as justice-involved individuals, families, and communities, and in forensic settings, including the courts, probation, prison, and reentry. Recent Council on Social Work Education (CSWE, 2015) revised accreditation standards, including building professional social workers' competencies in engaging in human rights and social, economic, and environmental justice, have opened a new doorway for contemporary professionals, such as social workers and lawyers, such as Maren Willins and Ashley Ratliff, to share their field-generated knowledge in working collaboratively to assist criminal justice-involved individuals and families in the criminal justice system, especially the courts.

Since the birth of the profession of social work over 120 years ago, frontline forensic social workers practiced at the intersection of social services and the legal system. These early pioneers understood that frontline social workers can and should be actively involved in providing social services, but they can and should also be involved in government, working for policy reform. Their efforts in the justice system, especially the criminal justice system, have set a high standard for the forensic social workers of today. Our foremothers saw that advocating for their "clients" meant advocating for systemic reform as they collaborated to apply a two-pronged approach to social welfare: individual and social change. These early efforts of friendly visitors and settlement of house workers have laid the ground for 21st-century forensic social workers to further develop an integrated approach to practice, especially related to a historically overlooked population of individuals, families, and communities directly impacted by the criminal justice system (Maschi, Leibowitz, & Killian, 2018).

The history of forensic social work is difficult to separate from the history of social work itself. In fact, one of social work's first professional societies was the National Conference of Charities and Corrections, formed in 1879—pioneer social worker Jane Addams became the leader of the organization in 1909. This suggests the importance given to corrections, both in early conceptualizations of social services formed over a century ago and in today's understanding of the proper venues for social workers as actors and advocates. To trace the history of forensic social work, we need to look first at the history of forensic policy in the North American colonies and then at the creation of social work and the introduction of social workers to carry out or change those policies (Maschi et al., 2018). For a more detailed history of forensic social work, see Maschi, Leibowitz, and Killian at http://www.springerpub.com/media/samplechapters/9780826120663/9780826120663_chapter.pdf.

In these exciting contemporary times, in the new book by Maren Willins and Ashley Ratliff entitled *Criminal Defense-Based Forensic Social Work*, the roles, skills, and team approach model is creating a new chapter in forensic social work history. The book gives social workers practical tips on how to navigate the legal system, collaborating from within the system for justice for individuals, families, and communities. Madden (2003) stresses the point, "If the social work profession is to be in control of its future, it must become committed to the role of exerting influence on the legal system through education, advocacy and proactive legal policy development" (pp. 3–4). This book will assist social workers with the knowledge, values, and skills to do just that. This book speaks to both forensic social work and collaboration with sister professions, such as that of the lawyers using the central guiding conceptual models of social work practice: a human rights, social justice, and person-in-environment perspective, along with social systems theories. These are the critical skills and training that social workers are able to bring to the criminal defense team table.

Criminal defense-based forensic social work also illustrates how social workers respond to individuals in the criminal justice system and work to change the system in which such individuals find themselves. Moreover, there are many examples on how social workers and interdisciplinary partners not only respond to individuals affected by state and federal laws but also work to change those laws. Forensic social work, especially criminal defense-focused forensic social work, is as old as social work itself, and it represents the full diversity of our profession, which includes advocating for those accused or convicted of a crime, standing up for victims, responding to youth in juvenile justice systems, testifying in court on behalf of both litigants and defendants, supporting and working alongside law enforcement professionals, and working to improve or change the processes and policies of the United States justice system. This book, written by professionals in the field, shows exactly how this can be done.

How could forensic social work not be present in arenas such as the criminal justice system, especially the courts? As Maschi, Leibowitz, and Killian (2018) have underscored, our profession revolves around social justice and human rights. Throughout United States history, social justice (and, in later years, global and universal human rights) has been the core of the theory and practice of social work. Social workers stand for those who cannot; speak for those who have been silenced; and seek to create conditions of empowerment for individuals, families, and communities. Willins and Ratliff's model provides readers how social workers "do it" in the courts.

Forensic social workers have practice specialty areas, such as criminal defense-based social work, where they can concentrate their individual and collective efforts toward advancing human rights. These areas include practice and systems reform in legal settings that address and redress, juvenile justice, criminal justice, health care, immigration, mental health, victims' rights, and civil rights for racial-ethnic and homosexual minorities. For example, forensic social workers whose efforts are focused on juvenile and criminal justice human rights reform can advocate for the rights of offenders of all ages detained in penal institutions, the rights of minorities disproportionately involved in the criminal justice system, the rights of criminal offenders to rehabilitation and training, the rights of children born to women prisoners, the rights of juvenile prisoners, the rights of political prisoners, the rights of probationers, and the rights of those sentenced to capital punishment. There is also the potential to greatly improve the dehumanizing aspects of prison, including improving prison conditions themselves and improving community conditions, such as living in poverty and crime-ridden neighborhoods, that place people at risk of engaging in criminal offenses (United Nations, 1994; Wronka, 2008).

Willins and Ratliff's groundbreaking book is consistent with the specialization of forensic social work and serves as an ideal vehicle for navigating the sociolegal (i.e., social and legal) environment that goes beyond social work practice as usual. It offers an integrative practice model that incorporates social work ethics, generalist and specialist practice, and the knowledge and skills of research as well as the nature of evidence, law, policy practice, and interdisciplinary or interprofessional and intersectoral collaboration in criminal defense. In fact, the authors in this text demonstrate a commitment to practice that involves psychosocial and legal interventions, and is consistent with the historic two-pronged integrated approach to social work practice.

As described in this book, Willins and Ratliff demonstrate how their contemporary forensic practices use a two-pronged approach to facilitate change: (a) assisting individuals and families to improve functioning and (b) combating unjust and unfair community and societal conditions through strategies of social reform (Bartlett, 1958). These strategies are explained in the mission statement of the National Association of Social Workers Code of Ethics (2017), in which a historic and defining feature of the social work profession is "individual well-being in a social context and the well-being of society" (NASW, 2017). Central to the social work mission is consideration of the "environmental forces that create, contribute, and address problems in living" (NASW).

Also, as demonstrated in this book, the authors show how criminal defense forensic social work targets their interventions at the micro level (e.g., individuals), the mezzo level (e.g., families and groups), and/or the macro level (e.g., institutions, organizations, cultures, communities, and society) (Zastrow & Kirst-Ashman, 2012). Miley, O'Meila, and Dubois (2012) outlined four major goals for practice addressing multilevel assessment and intervention strategies. These four goals are:

1 Enhancing people's individual functioning, problem-solving, and coping abilities
2 Linking clients to needed resources
3 Working to develop and improve the social-service delivery network
4 Promoting social justice through the development of social policy.

Also demonstrated is that the social environment is often viewed as the place in which person-in-environment interactions occur (Zastrow & Kirst-Ashman, 2012). However, although the social environment is commonly viewed as omnipresent, the justice environment that is informed by human rights is equally present. The justice environment consists of individuals, families, and communities seeking freedom from oppression, fairness, equality, and the balance of power as well as the laws, policies, and legal system that affect the social environment (Barker, 2003). There are many examples in the text that illustrate how the law, with its legal rules and mandates, should be viewed as a mechanism that frames social work practice (Madden, 2003).

Maschi and colleagues (2018) proposed a social justice systems theoretical model that conceptualized the interaction of persons within a "social justice" environment, such as those impacted by the criminal legal system. Social workers and their professional collaborators must manage both the social and legal (aka sociolegal), that is, the social justice (person-in-environment interactions that seek a balance toward social justice or fairness) and the legal environment (which represents the law, the legal process, and institutions that seek individual and community protection). The Colorado Model presented by Willins and Ratliff provides copious examples of how this can be done.

Social workers also must recognize that individuals and families may be involved in multiple systems concurrently or sequentially (Garland, Hough, Landsverk & Brown, 2001; Maschi et al., 2018). For example, an adolescent who has been involved in the Department of Human Services (DHS) as a foster child may also find themselves in the juvenile justice system because he has been charged in a gang-related offense. This adolescent may have various professionals, both social workers and attorneys, involved in his life as case managers, defense attorneys, forensic social workers, and possibly a Guardian et Liteum (GAL).

This book fills a gap in the field of forensic scholarship generated from front-line practitioners. I highly recommend it. It is a much-needed resources for new and seasoned forensic social workers to learn from experienced social workers, lawyers, and other professionals on how to navigate criminal defense social work, especially in the court system. The book also has relevance to social workers in other settings who collaborate with those in the juvenile or criminal court systems. As social workers, the pursuit of justice seems to be in our DNA. Reading and applying the lessons learned in this book will assist new and seasoned social workers in putting their justice DNA into action.

REFERENCES

Council on Social Work Education [CSWE]. (2015). *Educational Policy and Accreditation Standards (EPAs)*. Alexandria, VA: Author.

Garland, A.F., Hough, R.L., Landsverk, J.A., & Brown, S.A. (2001). Multi-sector complexity of systems of care for youth with mental health needs. *Children's Services: Social Policy, Research and Practice*, *4*, 123–140.

Madden, R., & Wayne, R.H. (2003). Social work and the law: A therapeutic jurisprudence perspective. *Social Work*, *48*, 338–347.

Maschi, T., & Leibowitz, G. (2018). *Forensic social work: A psychosocial legal approach to diverse criminal justice populations and settings* (2nd ed.). New York, NY: Springer Publishing.

Miley, K.K., O'Melia, M.O., & DuBois, B. (2012). *Generalist social work practice: An empowering approach* (7th ed.). Boston, MA: Pearson Education.

National Association of Social Workers. (2017). *Code of ethics of the National Association of Social Workers*. Washington, DC: NASW Press.

Zastrow, C.H., & Kirst-Ashman, K.K. (2012). *Understanding human behavior and the social environment* (9th ed.). Belmont, CA: Brooks/Cole-Thompson Learning.

PREFACE

Colorado Model of Criminal Defense-Based Forensic Social Work

Ashley Ratliff and Jacoba Rock

In the fall of 2012, I, Ashley Ratliff, JD, MSW, met a young man, a barely 18-year-old, frail teenager who was in the medical unit of the local jail. His anxiety was palpable. Immediately, I knew that it was going to take a longer visit than planned to fully explain to him the first-degree murder charges he faced from a situation that had occurred when he was 17 and the possible penalty of spending his life in prison. His first question to me was "When can I go back to high school?" His focus on this goal was incredibly naïve but persistent and honorable. It took several visits to help him understand his charges and the potential impact to his future, resulting from one evening when he almost died during a fistfight-turned-gunfight among four juveniles. Shortly before this meeting, I had also been appointed to represent a different young man who had been sentenced to life in prison for violent offenses that had occurred in the late 1990s; because of significant changes in constitutional law regarding cruel and unusual punishments for juveniles, his case was going to get a second look in the courts. This individual was so anxious about his circumstances that he would be physically ill prior to my visiting with him. My commitment to representing the legal needs of these two young men brought about feelings of gratitude for my Master of Social Work (MSW) degree and my ability to recognize the need for a comprehensive, client-centered team approach that would allow me to better represent each young person as more than their criminal behaviors. This professional team approach would hopefully lead to effective advocacy for these deserving individuals and others facing serious criminal charges and consequences or those who were told they would die in prison for crimes they had committed as children. The latter group of incarcerated offenders, convicted and sentenced to Juvenile Life in Prison Without Parole (JLWOP) for crimes committed when they were juveniles, were now facing the possibility of returning to their families and communities, and their legal teams were tasked with showing the Court and other decision-makers how their reentry could be successful and safe.

In the fall of 2012, I, Jacoba Rock, LCSW, was working with a group of Guardian *ad litem* (GAL) attorneys, appointed to represent the best interests of children (ages 0–18 years) involved in Dependency and Neglect cases as part of a new multidisciplinary model of partnerships between attorneys and social workers. I had also been facilitating high-risk restorative justice dialogue for several years. Despite their challenging life circumstances, my favorite clients were those teenagers who were attempting to overcome years of abuse, neglect, and system involvement, to use their voices and behaviors to fight for their futures. Many of these young people were part of a particularly high-risk population, what research has identified as "crossover youth" or "dual-systems youth," court-involved youth who have a history of trauma, identified by the system or not, or those young people simultaneously involved in both the child welfare and juvenile and/or criminal justice systems (Widom & Maxfield, 2001; Halemba et al., 2004). I was often inspired by the resilience of these young individuals and curious about the narratives and pathways which had led them from trauma experiences to delinquency involvement; furthermore, I could not imagine anyone more deserving of the best advocacy and services necessary to experience positive life changes. I was approached by the talented Ms. Ratliff to collaborate with her on one of her early JLWOP cases, a young person who had faced such adversity, and unbeknownst to us at the time, the Colorado Model of criminal defense-based forensic social work was born. What occurred next was profound and has become an invaluable team approach to representing the most vulnerable youth and young adults in juvenile and criminal court proceedings.

A couple acknowledgments must be made here about the emergence of our model. First, several excellent Public Defense offices (the Maryland Office of the Public Defender, the Equal Justice Initiative, the District of Columbia Legal Services, and the Bronx Defenders, to name a few) and juvenile law clinics (such as those at Northwestern University and Boston College) had already been using interdisciplinary collaborations between social workers and attorneys to both successfully advocate for and support court-involved young people. Though the specific tasks carried out by these social worker and attorney teams may be different, the idea that the best representation may happen through collaboration is not new. After we began to develop our program, we often interfaced with attorneys and social workers from these other agencies and benefited from their guidance and feedback; among other goals, we hope that this book will provide a framework for us to continue to engage in dialogue about how best to serve clients through interdisciplinary collaborations. Taking another step back, social workers have been effectively employed as capital (death penalty) mitigation specialists for many years. We acknowledge that collaboration and interdisciplinary approaches to criminal defense are critical and form a foundation for best practices in zealous defense of vulnerable populations; similarly, social workers value interdisciplinary collaborations to meet the multitude of needs for clients. Second, there were relatively few social workers who worked with offenders when this model emerged—and some stigma around this area of social work practice—though a growing acknowledgment of the match between social work skills and knowledge, and the needs of the criminal offender population in terms of advocacy, assessment, and treatment. We are grateful for the social workers who pioneered clinical and community work with criminal and juvenile offenders, many of them operating for years prior to the establishment of this model, often lone voices in a sea of more traditional, punitive, and deficit-minded justice system practitioners.

Across the country, in the wake of *Graham v. Florida* (2010), soon followed by *Miller v. Alabama (2012)*, over 2,000 inmates' futures became uncertain because they were eligible for resentencing—these were juveniles sentenced to life in prison, and those sentences were deemed unconstitutional. In Colorado, there were approximately 50–100 inmates whose cases were identified as having been impacted by this new constitutional jurisprudence around juvenile sentencing under adult mandatory sentencing schemes. Because of the efforts of the CJDC, a local nonprofit agency in Colorado dedicated to ensuring excellence in juvenile defense, coordination of advocates at the center of this realm of legal practice quickly became a priority. The CJDC's mission is to ensure high standards of practice in juvenile defense through training, resources, and a robust policy center—and through this agency, several litigation committees were created. In close partnership with national colleagues and organizations, Ms. Ratliff helped establish litigation committees at CJDC for advocates representing children facing adult prosecution and those serving unconstitutional sentences to come together to brainstorm a myriad of legal issues as well as to provide training and research databases for attorneys and advocates working closely with this population. What became clear was the need for an expert on defense teams to (1) assist these young individuals as they grappled with the uncertainty of their future lives and to (2) help defense attorneys compile comprehensive mitigation investigations, support healthy and safe client functioning, and create viable reentry plans. A central role became the telling of the incredible narratives of each of these youth, many of these stories previously untold due in part to the severe mandatory waiver and harsh sentencing practices in place since a conservative juvenile justice law and policy reform in the mid-1990s.

Collaboration on the initial JLWOP case that we worked on together led to a quick discovery of previously unidentified and unaddressed traumas of the client, significant systemic failure, needs for family engagement and cultural humility, challenges to help the client balance feelings of hopefulness and hopelessness, and related needs for strong professional boundaries; simply put, there were a multitude of needs on this case and others that defense attorneys may not have always been trained in but needs that many attorneys working on the cases recognized and desired to meet. After recognizing this need, we were able to develop this team approach to working with some of our most vulnerable clients, with invaluable guidance and support from several agencies, and specifically because of the resources, space, and backing provided by the CJDC, an internship was created in close partnership with two local graduate school programs.

This unique model of holistic, client-centered defense has provided invaluable support for many clients, beginning with our most vulnerable populations—individuals who as juveniles were convicted and sentenced as adults, in addition to children facing adult prosecution. Building from the theoretical frameworks of Psychosocial Development (Erikson, 1960), Ecological Systems (Bronfenbrenner, 1989), and Risk and Resilience (Masten, 2001), as well as narrative and social justice orientations, this comprehensive, developmentally informed model employs a *past* (i.e., mitigation themes and life history compilation), *present* (i.e., client contact and current functioning support), and *future* (i.e., reentry services and/or least restrictive placement advocacy) framework. It combines records, interviews, and social science research to identify unmet needs and historical influences on a young person's path over time. In addition, to support a young client facing extreme uncertainty, our model focuses on one-on-one work with each client to help them improve their daily life and to build skills that can be used in the reentry process. Finally, social workers develop a plan for the future by addressing unmet needs and risks, as well as building on identified strengths and sources of support, toward a comprehensive reentry plan. Within each of these realms, significant family and community engagement takes place which enhances future potential tremendously.

We appreciate the hard work of all of the attorneys, investigators, and social workers that supported the inception of this model through collaboration on cases, brainstorming and development meetings, and beyond. We are particularly indebted to the high level of clinical skills, passion, and commitment of the MSW interns and entry-level social workers who first applied for the roles we advocated for; the many legal advocates and leaders who supported this work; the university systems that provided us with guidance and support through internships; and, of course, the clients themselves, who were largely willing to try a new and relatively unheard of model of working with our interdisciplinary defense teams. We recognize that no one can do this work alone and further that the growth of this model has not been without barriers or opportunities for learning. We ourselves have evolved exponentially since beginning our collaborative work on that first case. Both of us have continued as social work educators: Ms. Rock has returned to a doctoral program to complete research on the crossover youth trajectory, and Ms. Ratliff continues to fight for individuals facing extreme sentences or serving unconstitutional life sentences as well as providing expert consultations and extensive trainings on this model to support many criminal defense teams across Colorado and the country.

The Colorado Model of criminal defense-based forensic social work has undertaken a unique approach to the best representation of our most vulnerable populations by joining forces of forensic social workers, attorneys, and other members of the criminal defense team. This holistic, client-centered collaboration has empowered many court-involved youth to have their voices be heard and to address their need to be treated fairly and their rights to make certain decisions about their cases and lives. These efforts have thus far proven to keep many youth in juvenile court, thwarting the negative consequences and trajectories of harsh sentencing and the dearth of treatment options in the adult criminal justice system. These innovations have far-reaching implications for all juvenile defense systems and their clients.

We were fairly quickly able to demonstrate the success of this model in and out of the courtroom as clients are more engaged and validated; legal advocacy efforts are more comprehensive; and, thus, lawyers scramble to make requests for social workers to work on their teams, particularly when they are working with clients who are young and/or have severe traumas, cognitive impairments, or mental health disorders. Excellent leadership continues in the growing number of agencies, firms, and partnerships that do this incredible work for and with their deserving clients in Colorado and across the United States; thank goodness because, in collaboration with our clients, we continue to be tasked with overcoming major obstacles in the legal system and beyond to realize justice and support reentry for those moving forward from incarceration. What began as our creative collaboration on one case has expanded to a variety of clients involved in the criminal court system whose attorneys seek to best represent a client facing juvenile and criminal court proceedings as well as assist with some clients' post-conviction/adjudication. We all remain as passionate as ever about "righting the wrongs" experienced by young people in trouble through excellence in holistic, client-centered advocacy and interdisciplinary partnerships between attorneys and social workers. By writing this book, we hope to inspire other professionals in their individual and collaborative efforts to seek innovative options to meet the needs of their clients and to provide a framework that guides social workers and attorneys in developing their roles and programs of criminal defense-based forensic social work practice. It is our honor and privilege to share this model with you here.

(Giselle Gutierrez-Ruiz, used with permission)

ACKNOWLEDGMENTS

The authors of this book would like to sincerely thank the following colleagues and supporters of this book and what has been accomplished. We could not have done it without those of you in the field alongside us, in the courtroom, in our offices, and on paper.

Our gratitude is immeasurable for the CJDC, where the work to start this model of practice began. Specifically, we wish to thank Kim Dvorchak, former executive director of CJDC, and Lindy Frolich, director of the Colorado Office of the Alternate Defense Counsel (OADC), who immediately embraced the idea to include social workers on defense teams and provided incredible support to this model and manner of practice, and have continuously supported evolution over the years.

Thank you to two other pioneers of this incredible work: Patti Puritz, former executive director of the National Juvenile Defender Center (NJDC), who recognized the power of a developmental framework for juvenile cases at the very beginning—long before the United States Supreme Court—and has continued to advocate for a compassionate understanding of each young person. Thank you also to juvenile defense attorney extraordinaire Simmie Baer, who is the record holder for number of compelling developmental presentations of adolescents in juvenile and adult courts in Washington, Illinois, and Colorado.

Lastly, we would like to acknowledge several experts in the field whose input from the day we started our work in Colorado through to the writing of this book has been invaluable. Tina Maschi, PhD, of Fordham University, the leading expert in forensic social work, not only provided tremendous insights for us but also authored the foreword that starts this book with incredible history in the making. We are also grateful to the reviewers of our original idea and manuscript proposal and of this book, including Lori James-Townes, LCSW; Maria Morrison, LCSW of Equal Justice Initiative (EJI); Robin Dickerhoof of

Red Ink Editing Services; and Kimberly Bender, PhD, social work professor at the University of Denver (DU).

Finally, this book could not have been possible without the love and support of our families and the inspiration of our clients.

Maren Willins
Ashley Ratliff
Hillary Vervalin
Claire Schmidt
Molly Hennessey
Kathy Maquire
Sarah Buchanan
Marty Beyer
Tina Maschi
Jacoba Rock

ABOUT THE CONTRIBUTORS

Tina Maschi, PhD, LCSW, ACSW, is an associate professor and researcher at Fordham University's Graduate School of Social Service. She is a licensed clinical social worker and has over 30 years of practice and research experience working with diverse populations in criminal justice settings, including prisons. She is author and/or editor of four books, including *Forensic Social Work: Psychosocial Legal Aspects Across Diverse Populations and Settings* (2nd ed.).

Marty Beyer, PhD, is an independent national juvenile justice and child welfare consultant. Her work focuses on the impact of cognitive, moral, and identity development; trauma and disabilities on youth offenses; Miranda; competency; and rehabilitation planning. Dr. Beyer began utilizing a developmental framework early in her career in delinquency programs and has been teaching her Developmental Assessment approach to social workers, lawyers, and judges for many years. She helped juvenile justice systems implement Youth Family Team Meetings, developed a policy and staff training regarding the treatment of LGBT youth in Hawaii, designed a plan for girls in the Connecticut juvenile justice system, and recently completed her work as the United States Department of Justice Mental Health Monitor in juvenile facilities in New York. She also assisted with the statewide implementation of strengths-/needs-based child welfare practice in Alabama and Oregon, and litigation in Massachusetts to secure Medicaid-funded intensive home-based services for children in the juvenile justice, child welfare, and mental health systems, and is supporting mental health services for children in foster care in LA. Dr. Beyer has a PhD in clinical psychology from Yale University. Her articles can be found on her website www.MartyBeyer.com.

Ashley Ratliff, JD, MSW, has been a juvenile defense attorney, both within the Colorado Office of the State Public Defender and as an independent contractor with Alternate Defense Counsel, for over 10 years. She is an expert in comprehensive holistic child-centered litigation for children prosecuted in adult and juvenile courts. She currently leads the Youth in Adult Court Litigation Committee for the CJDC, which was instrumental in the 2012 legislative changes to the Direct File Statute and 2016 legislative changes to the sentencing/resentencing of juveniles accused of the most serious crimes in adult courts. Ms. Ratliff is an adjunct professor at the University of Denver's School of Social Work. She received her law degree from California Western School of Law simultaneous to receiving a Master of Social Work from San Diego State University in San Diego, California, in 2006. The focus of this dual degree program was on juvenile justice and child advocacy.

Jacoba Rock, LCSW, is a PhD candidate in the Human Development and Family Studies and Criminology programs at Pennsylvania State University. She studies the development of aggressive and delinquent behaviors in adolescence and young adulthood, particularly through empirical connections to earlier life experiences of trauma and moderating cognitive and psychosocial factors. She worked for many years as a Forensic Social Worker in both Colorado and Pennsylvania, and has been a Social Work and Criminology educator for both the University of Denver and Simmons College in Boston, Massachusetts. Combining her academic and practice experiences, Jacoba is particularly interested in the translation of biopsychosocial developmental research to intervention opportunities for high-risk youth and young adults involved in the criminal justice system.

Maren Willins, LCSW, is a criminal defense-based forensic social worker and psychotherapist in the Denver metro area. She is a licensed clinical social worker and has been working in the public and private criminal justice field for over 15 years. She has been a forensic social worker with the Alternate Defense Counsel in Colorado for 4 years and worked with the Public Defender's Office for 5 years. She passionately works on criminal defense-based teams to tell her clients' stories, to advocate for alternative and appropriate sentencing, and to advocate for mental health treatment. She has had her own psychotherapy private practice for over 10 years, in which she provides solution-focused and client-centered therapy for individuals as well as supervision to new social workers. Maren earned her graduate degree in social work and her undergraduate degree in psychology at Washington University in St. Louis.

Sarah Buchanan, PhD, LCSW, is a two-time graduate of the University of Tennessee and a graduate of the University of Michigan with bachelor's, master's, and doctoral degrees in social work. She is a licensed clinical social worker. Her interest in forensic social work developed when she was a student, prompting her to complete her field placements in various legal settings. She worked in community mental health in a rural Appalachian community before returning to public defense in 2012. Sarah's doctoral research focused on the impact of social work practice in public defense. Her research interests broadly include forensic social work and specifically include the integration of social workers into public defense systems.

Molly Hennessey, LSW, is a Licensed Social Worker in Colorado and currently practices as a public defense mitigation specialist in Seattle, Washington. She primarily works on public defense legal teams with juveniles and young adults charged with serious felonies. She completed her bachelor's degree in social work from Seattle University and went on to earn her master's degree in Social Work from the University of Denver. In graduate school, Molly completed a clinical track focusing on At Risk Youth and Interpersonal Trauma. Prior to moving home to Seattle, she began her career as a forensic social worker in Colorado. While there, she specialized in working on the legal teams of children charged as adults and adults serving JLWOP sentences. Molly is very passionate about working with youth, young adults, adults, and families involved with the legal system. In her work on defense teams, she utilizes a trauma-informed, strengths-based approach and regards clients as the experts on their life stories.

Hillary Vervalin, LCSW, is a licensed clinical social worker who holds a Master of Social Work from the University of Denver, with an emphasis on family systems and trauma-informed care. She has been a forensic social worker with the Alternate Defense Counsel in Colorado for 4 years and remains extremely passionate about combining social work skills, values, and ethics with work on criminal defense teams to provide client-centered, positive outcomes in juvenile, adult, and capital cases. She has testified as a forensic social worker in front of the Colorado General Assembly on two occasions in support of reform for JLWOP laws. She is also a founding member of the Chained Voices Art Committee, which provides incarcerated and formerly incarcerated artists with the chance to display and sell their art in the community. Hillary's experience includes assistant teaching at the University of Denver's Graduate School of Social Work as well as individual and family substance-abuse therapy with adult females and adolescents in both residential and outpatient settings. She was named the CJDC's Forensic Social Worker of the Year in 2016.

Kathy McGuire, JD, MSW, received her law degree from the University of Denver School of Law in 1994 and a master's degree in social work from the University of Wisconsin-Madison in 1985. Ms. McGuire has had a private law practice since 2013. Prior to this, she was a deputy state public defender for 19 years, spending 10 years as a trial deputy and 9 years as the manager of a regional trial office. She has represented thousands of adults and juveniles charged with criminal offenses; a large number of her clients have serious mental illnesses.

She has been a member of the Legislative Advisory Task Force for Persons with Mental Illness in the Criminal Justice System for approximately 8 years and was the Chair of this task force for 18 months. She was involved in the Drug Policy Task Force which advised the Colorado Criminal and Juvenile Justice Commission concerning modifications to offenses involving controlled substances. Ms. McGuire used her background in social work to write a grant for the Office of the Public Defender in the 1990s which led to the first social worker being hired by this statewide agency.

Claire Schmidt, LCSW, is a Denver-based Forensic Social Worker. She earned her Master of Social Work from Colorado State University. Before contracting with the Alternate Defense Counsel as a forensic social worker, she worked to empower, educate, and advocate with and for individuals living with HIV, survivors of domestic violence, and young people who identify as lesbian, gay, bisexual, transgender, queer or questioning, and intersex (LGBTQI). Claire is passionate about combing her experience in both clinical- and community-based social work with her growing practice as a member of criminal defense teams. Her practice is currently focused on recognizing the unique needs, challenges, and strengths of clients navigating the criminal justice system.

1

INTRODUCTION AND OVERVIEW

Ashley Ratliff and Marty Beyer

Each of us is more than the worst thing we've ever done.

Bryan Stevenson

All individuals charged with crimes are more than their worst acts. A myriad of factors in a person's life at various points in time contribute to their life course trajectory. Courts must be informed about the numerous developmental and historical factors contributing to an offense. This complex developmental story is essential to address the unmet needs of clients in juvenile and criminal court systems to achieve rehabilitative outcomes instead of purely punitive sanctions. To reveal the mitigating circumstances surrounding a client and their case, in addition to identifying the resources and supports necessary to help that individual move beyond their worst act, a client-centered holistic team approach to criminal defense is critical. The Colorado Model of Criminal Defense-Based Forensic Social Work is the approach of practitioners who came together to represent our most vulnerable clients and is a launching place for anyone working with clients in the juvenile or adult criminal court systems.

This introduction provides an overview of the principles that guided the authors to develop a model of holistic defense. The discussion will include the importance of trauma-informed developmental assessments and how forensic social workers are well suited to put together the critical narratives to inform decision-makers in achieving developmentally sound justice. The introduction will conclude with an overview of the chapters of this book as well as summaries of the case studies that bring the concepts of the book to life through fictional client examples.

Constitutional Jurisprudence—Framework for Inclusion of Developmental Science into the Law

Representation of children facing adult prosecution as well as young men and women serving unconstitutional sentences is a unique and specialized area of practice that led the authors to design this model of criminal defense-based forensic social work. The infusion of developmental science into criminal cases began most distinctly when the United States Supreme Court abolished the death penalty as a punishment for children in *Roper vs. Simmons*, 543 U.S. 551 (2005). Here, the Court acknowledged three distinct attributes of youth that mitigate culpability: (1) developmentally; the hallmark features of adolescence/youth involve risk-taking, impetuosity, and a failure to appreciate risks and consequences; (2) youth are more susceptible to outside pressures—such as from peers or family members—and have limited ability to remove themselves from the settings which may contribute to an offense; and (3) youth's identities or characters are not yet formed and thus have a tremendous capacity for change (Steinberg, 2014). Brain development research suggests that development is ongoing until the mid-20s (American Psychological Association, Amici curiae brief, *Miller v. Alabama*, United States Supreme Court, 2012). In 2010, the Court took the principles of developmental research further and reaffirmed the critical differences between youth and adults based in brain science to abolish the sentence of life without parole for juvenile offenders who were convicted of "nonhomicide" crimes. In *Graham v. Florida*, the Court held "that for a juvenile offender who did not commit homicide the Eighth Amendment forbids the sentence of life without parole" (*Graham v. Florida*, 2010). Specifically, the Court held "that the Eighth Amendment forbids a sentencing scheme that mandates life in prison without the possibility of parole for juvenile offenders" (*Graham*, 2016). Because youth matters under the Constitution, individualized sentencing that considers youthfulness and other mitigating factors is required by the Eighth Amendment.

For over a decade, the United States Supreme Court has validated and confirmed in the cases of *Roper*, *Graham*, and *Miller* that young people are different from adults, that youth is always a mitigating factor, and that youth matters in determining culpability and disposition in court. Developmental research, neuroscience, and behavioral considerations guided these important cases. In the wake of these critical Court decisions, a more specialized field of practice evolved nationally around representing youth facing life sentences and for practitioners to use in resentencing hearings for those now serving unconstitutional life sentences imposed upon them as children. At the same time, in Colorado, significant changes to the laws surrounding the prosecution of youth in adult courts were also occurring. Legal frameworks were being developed at the legislature as well as provided through case law, and in order to best develop the necessary evidence for these legal factors, inclusion of a forensic social worker on the defense team was essential. While legal standards were evolving, the authors of this book—practitioners in the field working with clients facing resentencing hearings after decades in prison with no hope for release and representing juveniles at risk of adult court prosecution—developed this model of holistic client-centered representation with inclusion of forensic social workers. Criminal defense-based social work has led a movement toward developmentally sound justice around the country.

The Developmental Approach

Youth and young adults in juvenile and criminal courts are significantly impacted by their immaturity, most are shaped by trauma, and at least half are affected by disabilities. Their offenses, their peer connections, their relationships with family, their participation in school, their substance use, and their contact with professionals cannot be understood without appreciating their immature thinking, reactions to maltreatment and loss, and comprehension problems. A developmental approach is necessary to represent a client facing criminal charges. Systematically putting together the pieces behind a young person's actions is important in every case. The developmental factors that contributed to who the person was at the time of the offense are also the framework for rehabilitative services that address community safety. A developmental assessment weaves together immaturity, disabilities, and trauma to understand the young person's behaviors, relationships, and emotions to design effective rehabilitative services (Beyer, 2011).

For the incarcerated adult with an unconstitutional sentence, the application of a developmental framework retrospectively can contribute to assessment of readiness for release.

Developmental assessments began decades ago as a result of questions from courts that recognized that a young person cannot be defined simply by their offense. Courts wanted to know what unique combination of services would fit each young person developmentally and would provide effective rehabilitation. This question could not be answered by traditional court evaluations that rendered a diagnosis or presented the results of intelligence quotient (IQ) and personality testing. While psychological and psychiatric evaluations may summarize a young person's history, in recent years, it has been forensic social workers who have taken the lead in comprehensive developmental assessments. The biopsychosocial and ecological perspectives in the training and experience of forensic social workers make them uniquely skilled at telling a young person's story in a developmental context:

- Who was this young person at the time of the offense?
- What were his/her family relationships, school experience, and peer connections?
- What were the specific effects of past trauma, disabilities, and immaturity on his/her behavior at the time of the offense?
- What is required for her/him to be successful and give the community confidence in his/her minimal risk of reoffending?

Justice systems in the past utilized linear stage-based theories about adolescence. This outmoded view of development did not include the effects of trauma or the impact of learning difficulties on a young person, or the unique family and peer contexts of his/her behavior. Furthermore, recent teen brain studies have demonstrated that

> adolescents behave differently than adults because their minds operate differently, their emotions are more volatile, and their brains are anatomically immature...their brains are physiologically underdeveloped in the areas that control impulses, foresee consequences, and temper emotions. They handle information processing and the management of emotions differently from adults... Cognitive experts have shown that the difference between teenage and adult behavior is not the adolescent's inability to distinguish right from wrong... Rather, the difference lies in what scientists have characterized as deficiencies in the way adolescents think, an inability to perceive and weigh risks and benefits accurately... Adolescents are inherently more prone to risk-taking behavior and less capable of resisting impulses... Stress, emotions and peer pressure affect everyone's cognitive functioning, but they operate on the adolescent differently and with special force.
>
> *(American Medical Association, Amici curiae brief,* Roper v. Simmons, *United States Supreme Court, 2005, pp. 4–20)*

Overlooking this broader adolescent perspective, both in understanding the young person's behavior and in designing rehabilitative services, resulted in court decisions that often were not developmentally sound.

There is substantial research on the lasting effects of both disabilities and trauma on youth, and these are not compatible with the simplistic view that offending is a bad choice by a teen.

> What may be perceived as fixed personality traits in juveniles may in fact result from malleable factors such as present maturity level or social

> context, rather than ingrained or enduring aspects of personality or worldview. Research has shown that personality traits change significantly during the developmental transition from adolescence to adulthood.
>
> *(American Psychological Association, Amici curiae brief,* Miller v. Alabama, *United States Supreme Court, 2011, pp. 19–20)*

The notion that youth should control their actions does not recognize that teen behavior is reactive to past victimization and/or results from processing and executive function difficulties and/or immature thinking. Traumatized youth may not be able to make rational decisions when memories and anxiety from past maltreatment and loss are triggered. Youth with disabilities may not comprehend the choices in a stressful situation, especially when they are following others.

That maturity should be assessed as a distinct developmental characteristic has long been recognized by researchers but only recently considered in juvenile and criminal courts. Immaturity of thinking, planning, accurately seeing risks, and decision-making is characteristic of teenagers in general, often leading to consequences the young person did not anticipate and regrets. Studies over many years have concluded that adolescents think less maturely than adults, but justice systems treat teenagers as adults in many ways. Clinicians and educators recognize that each young person develops uniquely, with maturity, comprehension, and trauma recovery happening at a different and uneven pace for each individual. Traditional one-size-fits-all services—whether community-based or residential—are not likely to be effective, given the unique development of each teenager. Developmental assessment is a response to the interest of juvenile and criminal court judges in having a full picture of what was behind a young person's offense and what services are necessary to reduce the risk of reoffending and enable him/her to contribute to the community.

Furthermore, in presenting who the person was at the time of the offense, the forensic social worker includes family-, school-, and neighborhood-level risks and protections (the ecological approach). The client's current functioning, such as work and school achievements, daily living experiences, current social support, and other activities, are also presented. This information will contribute to the conclusion of the developmental assessment regarding what rehabilitative services will be effective so the client can be successful in reentry or toward remaining within the community.

The main components of a developmental assessment are immature thinking, immature identity, the effects of trauma, and the impact of disabilities.

<u>Immature thinking</u>: Young people have immature thought processes, including minimizing risks, not anticipating, reacting to stress, and seeing only one option. Their thinking is less mature when they are influenced by peers and/or under the influence of substances and/or not receiving sufficient adult supervision. Young people gradually develop mature moral reasoning but may

be incapable of applying their understanding of right and wrong, and responsibility when they are under stress or influenced by others.

Immature identity: Becoming good at something is the foundation for developing a strong, positive identity, which is a crucial task of adolescence. Many youth involved in the justice system have not experienced success and feel marginalized: Having an unformed identity makes them more vulnerable to involvement with delinquent peers and substance abuse. Furthermore, the development of a stable identity takes time, during which a young person needs approval from family and positive peers that justice-involved youth often do not receive.

The effects of trauma: Trauma—defined as not only sexual and physical abuse but also loss; disrupted caregiving; neglect; exposure to domestic and community violence; or being rejected due to race, ethnicity, sexual orientation, or gender identity—has lasting effects on child and adolescent development. Many youth involved in the justice system have not had effective trauma treatment, despite their known background of trauma. The continuing impact of past trauma on behavior has historically been underestimated. Teenagers with a history of trauma typically overreact emotionally, abuse substances, and have problems forming trusting relationships. Too often, symptoms of trauma have been blamed on the young person or misinterpreted as part of his/her character rather than a guide to what is behind behavior that can be changed.

The impact of disabilities: As many as half of the juvenile delinquent population, in comparison to less than 10% in the overall child population, have learning disabilities, including a variety of problems in listening, remembering, prioritizing, and strategizing as well as reading and math. Comprehension and executive function difficulties are common in delinquents and contribute to poor decision-making under stress leading up to an offense. Distractibility and impulsiveness evident in learning disabled young people may make them less able to stop behavior, which plays a role in delinquent behavior, especially when coupled with comprehension problems and immature thinking. Truancy in response to perceived criticism from teachers, bullying by classmates, and frustration with poor academic progress can begin early in learning disabled youth, and not attending school can lead to delinquency.

A developmental framework is not only crucial to understanding adolescents in juvenile and criminal court but also applicable to adults incarcerated for offenses when they were juveniles who are now eligible for resentencing as well as young adults facing charges in criminal court. Putting our clients' lives in a developmental context and identifying what is behind their behavior is crucial in advocating for their legal interests in every case. Forensic social workers are well qualified to thoroughly explore who the young person was developmentally at the time of the offense and provide that context to the defense team and the decision-makers—the state prosecutor, the jury, and the judge. Explaining their unique immaturity, effects of trauma, and disabilities can help the court understand their offense, assess future risk, and design rehabilitative services. Forensic social workers whose training and background stem from core principles of social work, systems theory, and the ecological perspective have the expertise critical to putting together a thorough developmental assessment and are invaluable members of any criminal defense team.

Forensic Social Workers on a Criminal Defense Team—A Critical Collaboration

Social workers can assist the defense team in understanding the context of immaturity, trauma, and disabilities behind the young person's relationships, success at school, and behavior prior to and during the offense. As criminal defense-based forensic social work has evolved, the social worker has been able to provide the defense team with a developmental framework for understanding the young person and presenting his/her story in court. In order to work together toward the best outcome for a client that addresses unmet needs and rehabilitation services, and provides a developmental history to the decision-maker, collaboration is a key factor for success at any level.

Criminal defense-based social work requires collaboration to provide comprehensive support to the client and the defense team. Collaboration within the field of forensic social work is supported by an ecological systems approach. A forensic social worker's ability to collaborate with the defense team and other systems overlapping with the legal system is essential in connecting clients with services that will address their immaturity, disabilities, and trauma as well as advocating for the best legal outcome for an individual client. Social workers on defense teams collaborate with clients, families, experts, detention facilities, and service providers to mitigate both direct and indirect harm.

Social workers have historically been integral members of defense teams in capital cases (cases where the state or federal prosecutor is seeking the death penalty). Today, their expertise is considered vital to any criminal or juvenile defense team because of the advanced clinical skills, training in systems theory, and ecological systems approaches that social workers utilize in working with clients (Guin, Noble, and Merrill, 2003; Schroeder, 2003). These skills have historically been found to be extremely useful in uncovering and interpreting the biopsychosocial realities of individuals charged with capital crimes (Schroeder et al., 2006). Similarly, social workers are well suited to uncover and interpret the developmental history and behavior of any person charged with a crime—juvenile or adult.

> The social worker is the logical professional to develop the initial social history, because he or she is educated to achieve a holistic perspective and

> is trained in interviewing and therapeutic skills. Those skills help her or him uncover many of the defendant's pertinent life experiences and give a balanced interpretation of how those life experiences are explained by current theory and human behavior research.
>
> *(Guin et. al, 2003; Andrews, 1991, p. 365)*

A criminal defense team that includes a forensic social worker can best provide the court or prosecutor with multiple perspectives, which

> results in a picture of the defendant as the center of ever-widening concentric circles of influence (that is, defendant, family, neighborhood, school, community, society), each one having factors and stressors that, interacting with each other, affect human development and behavior.
>
> *(Guin et. al, 2003, p. 363; Miller, 1995)*

The inclusion of social workers on criminal defense teams is critical. This collaboration is nationally recognized as efforts are being made to push toward a more holistic model of representation of persons charged with crimes in many states. "Social Work is an integral component of the model, providing the [Social Work] profession with a tremendous opportunity to influence the criminal justice system and better serve a population with which the profession has long claimed allegiance" (Buchannan & Nooe, 2017).

The guiding principles outlined earlier are what inspired the practitioners and authors of this book to create a model of holistic client-centered work with persons accused of crimes. Generally, this model of defense-based forensic social work began with a framework of considering a client through the following lenses:

- **Past**, including mitigation and social history compilation and an exploration of the client's development in a trauma-informed manner.
- **Present**, including current functioning and tools for skill building.
- **Future**, including reentry, alternatives to sentencing, treatment, and goals to become a productive citizen.

The background, training, and expertise graduate-level social workers possess is the natural fit for engaging with clients in this manner. Furthermore, forensic social workers contribute to a more comprehensive developmental approach in criminal defense practice. Over the years, the framework and growth of this model has been profound. The authors welcome further collaboration and research toward the representation of all clients within the criminal or juvenile court systems through a holistic team approach while working toward developmentally sound justice.

FIGURE 1.1 Past, Present, and Future

Utilizing the Colorado Model of Criminal Defense-Based Forensic Social Work as a starting place, forensic social workers work with clients and litigation teams to fashion multifaceted mitigation. This process involves developing comprehensive biopsychosocial assessments, time lines, and family and social histories; working closely with each client throughout the proceedings, paying special attention to their unique needs; and engaging in reentry planning in collaboration with family and community partners that provide viable avenues for skill building. This client-centered, developmental approach has empowered court-involved youth to have their voices heard and recognized their need to be treated fairly and their right to make certain decisions about their cases. Putting the client in a developmental context in various ways has kept youth in juvenile court and reduced adult sentencing. The innovations in the Colorado Model of Criminal Defense-Based Social Work team approach have far-reaching implications for all defenders and all clients facing criminal charges.

Overview of this Book

This book aims to provide students, social workers, defenders, and others working in juvenile and criminal court with a holistic client-centered approach. We envision this book being used for teaching in graduate schools of social work, law school programs which have clinics or direct practice components to legal studies, and defender agencies who contract with or employ social workers on staff. The book begins with a summary of practice standards, ethical considerations, and legal frameworks which guided the authors in the initial stages of this work. Additionally, several chapters are dedicated to the unique roles and skills that a forensic social worker brings to the criminal defense team and a look at some specialized skills within this unique collaborative effort. Four case studies of fictional clients are woven throughout the chapters to provide examples and highlight important aspects of criminal defense-based forensic social work.

In Chapter 2, "Guiding Principles of Practice," the authors identify several legal frameworks and guidelines toward the implementation of the Colorado Model of Criminal Defense-Based Social Work. This chapter explores a brief history of the roles in criminal justice that social workers have traditionally served and how this is an ever-evolving field of practice. The commonalities between legal ethics and social work ethics will be presented, followed by areas of potential pitfalls. Examples of these potential pitfalls will be discussed, with suggestions on how an employee model-based agency might anticipate and handle these situations when they arise. At the writing of this book, criminal defense-based social work is a newer field of practice. Therefore, long-term studies need to be conducted in order to further develop standards of practice.

Chapter 3, "Roles of the Forensic Social Worker," identifies many key roles of a criminal defense-based social worker in supporting a client and defense team. A primary role is finding the balance of client-determination and the goals of the attorney(s) representing the client. The forensic social worker supports the client during the legal case to assist the legal team in the goal of obtaining the best possible legal outcome for the client.

Chapter 4, "Skills," provides an overview of the many skills a forensic social worker brings to a team through their background and training as a social worker. The skill set includes knowledge and abilities at the clinical, community, and academic and multidisciplinary levels. Clinically, a forensic social worker must be able to connect and build rapport with an array of clients in community and facility settings, identify clinically relevant information, and inform nonclinical entities of relevancy to client and setting. Likewise, while not a therapist, a forensic social worker must also be able to work with clients to encourage skills including but not limited to mindfulness, anger management, cognitive behavioral modifications, and conflict resolution. This type of skill building with clients requires the forensic social worker to be aware of what clinical techniques are validated by research in order to provide evidence-based support to clients. Due to the varied nature locations in which forensic social workers practice, it is also important that they be able to modify and adjust clinical interventions to nonclinical settings. A forensic social worker must be knowledgeable about different community resources available to clients while incarcerated, upon reentry into the community, and/or if placed in treatment as an alternative to incarceration. Additionally, a forensic social worker must possess an understanding of criminological theory, practice, and risk and protective factors that are important in the criminal justice system. A forensic social worker must be able to bridge the gap between sociological models and criminological practice to encourage more positive client and system outcomes.

After these two chapters on the roles of the forensic social worker and core skills, a more in-depth look at specific skills is laid out in subsequent chapters. In Chapter 5, "Cultural Humility and Special Populations," we take a close look at these important concepts and the individual identities of our clients' that play a role in case conceptualization and mitigation presentation. It is essential for the criminal defense-based social worker to have cultural humility and ongoing training on the different identities our clients have. A forensic social worker with cultural humility will benefit their client by being able to show understanding of concerns that stem from systemic oppression as well as through their ability to address issues that the client faces on a day-to-day basis. Cultural competence and cultural humility include more than just an understanding of a client's race or ethnicity. Identities are multifaceted, and cultural humility considerations must include the client's sexual orientation, intellectual challenges, age, and social identities (gangs, socioeconomic status (SES), etc.), to name a few. The authors in this section will take a close look at some of the identified special populations we work with in the criminal defense field.

Another skill of forensic social workers is providing a defense team with various work products. A forensic social worker pulls together vast amounts of information from a variety of sources to inform the legal team and aid in the theory of mitigation for the case. Chapter 6, "Work Product," covers some of the most common work products for the legal team, which include session notes and reports from mitigation interviews. Session notes document important information from visits with a client in order to keep the legal team updated. A report from a mitigation interview is an objective documentation of what an individual who has information about the client's life history shared during an interview. Work products also include efforts made on behalf of a client to aid in the theory of mitigation for the case. This type of product can take on visual, written, or oral forms. The most common examples include but are not limited to biopsychosocial assessments, time lines, genograms, and eco-maps. The aforementioned work products can be used together or separately to better tell the client's story. Work products may also include oral presentations or court testimonies that serve to advocate for a certain outcome for the client.

Additionally, collaboration with experts outside of the defense team is a critical component of criminal defense-based social work. Clients' legal cases often have an array of issues that require collaboration with professionals who are qualified to consult on such issues. In Chapter 7, "Forensic Social Work and Collaboration with Expert Witnesses," the authors discuss identifying potential experts, hiring an expert and the collaborative process between the social worker and client, as well as the partnership between the social worker and the expert. Consultation with a qualified expert can assist with a more comprehensive defense of a client while also enhancing a foundation of credibility with prosecutors and the courts.

Last, but certainly not least, is a final chapter that focuses on self-care, where the authors provide some practical considerations for those in the field, with ideas to ensure we are our best selves when working with persons charged with crimes in the manner described, which is often stressful for us as professionals. In order for our work and ourselves to be at our best, we provide some strategies and tips for the reader to implement in their daily practices.

Case Studies

Throughout the book, case examples are provided to help the reader understand the topics. Each case study is fiction, created from the collective minds of the writers of this book. The four case studies illustrate various social work themes present in a variety of criminal defense-based forensic social work cases. While not every issue in working with our clients is included in these case studies, the major themes are presented. The four case studies will be referenced by each fictional client's name throughout the chapters of the book and in some chapters will be more thoroughly reintroduced.

Case Study #1 (Ben)

Ben is a 22-year-old male with symptoms of severe anxiety, including difficulty concentrating, racing thoughts, heart palpitations, sleep problems, nightmares, and weight loss. These symptoms started when he entered jail about 2 months ago. Ben has a history of experiencing similar symptoms of anxiety in his teenage years but never received a formal mental health diagnosis. You suspect that Ben is suffering from generalized anxiety disorder related to past and current trauma. Ben is not taking any medications and has no other medical concerns.

Ben's charges are kidnapping, theft of a motor vehicle, and second-degree manslaughter. When he was 16-years old, Ben was in juvenile court for two Driving While Impaired offenses, truancy, and misdemeanor trespassing. His current charges are Ben's first felonies. The incident that Ben was arrested for revolves around an alleged gang house party. During this party, a vehicle was stolen, and a male victim sustained serious bodily injury and died in the hospital 2 days after he was admitted.

You know that Ben originally got involved in a gang (the Bloods) because of his father, who is an Original Gangster (more commonly referred to as OG). Ben was jumped at age 14. He grew up in poverty and around pervasive community violence. You do not yet know the extent of violence and trauma that Ben was exposed to, but you suspect that there is a significant amount. While there is nothing in the medical records about traumatic brain injury (TBI), you suspect that Ben has had at least two concussions. Ben's parents were married shortly after his birth and divorced when Ben was 10 years old. He has two younger siblings, aged 18 and 14. Their father is married to Ben's mom.

Ben is not married and has no children. Ben completed his High School Equivalency Certificate (GED) at age 20 and has some work experience in the fast food industry. He has an interest in the culinary arts and aspires to move further in this field. Ben's father was also arrested on charges related to this incident. Ben's mother visits Ben in jail weekly.

Ben's attorneys would like you to provide emotional support to Ben while he is incarcerated, assess his mental health needs, and work with him and the jail to provide mental health treatment. Additionally, the attorneys would like you to explore his family, community, academic, medical, psychological, and employment history, and conceptualize it into a court report.

Case Study #2 (Deb)

Deb is a 30-year-old, African American female with a developmental disability and an IQ of 65. She is originally from an impoverished neighborhood in Detroit, Michigan. She and her mother moved to Colorado when Deb was 14 years old to get distance from some of their other family members. Deb was briefly married at age 18 years and divorced 2 years later. She has no children but has a dog she cares for by feeding him, walking him, and keeping him healthy. Deb has not completed high school and quit going to school at age 16. Deb has a history of theft; most of her charges were relatively minor, without any jail time. Currently, she violated her probation because she is having difficulty keeping track of her court and probation appointments. After her most recent arrest, Deb lost her job at the grocery store where she has worked for the past 5 years.

Deb is working with the same attorney who helped her during her previous legal issues 2 years ago. Her attorney secured a Personal Recognizance bond for Deb, who is currently living at her mother's house. Deb has been living with her aging mom, who is an alcoholic, for all of her life. Deb's attorney would like you to help Deb find more appropriate housing and "whatever else she needs."

Deb has various school and medical records that her attorney would like you to review. It will not only be important to obtain records for Deb, but individualized education program (IEP) records will provide greater details about her specific learning and developmental difficulties. As you review these records, you learn that several times during her childhood, the Department of Human Services (DHS) investigated alleged abuse against Deb by her mother's boyfriend at the time. You know from the DHS records that one of Deb's mom's boyfriends sexually abused Deb for about 8 months when she was 11 years old. Deb's school records reveal that she was in special education since kindergarten and connected with the Arc, an agency devoted to assisting people with intellectual and developmental disabilities, beginning at 8 years old.

When you first meet with Deb at her mother's house, you smell alcohol on her mother. She excused herself and stayed in her room for the remainder of your visit. After explaining who you are and your role as a forensic social worker, Deb asks, "Do you want to hear about when my mom's boyfriend had sex with me?"

Case Study #3 (Rodrigo)

Rodrigo is a 16-year-old male who experienced significant abuse and neglect in the foster care system as a child. He was separated from his brother at the age of 3, and they grew up moving frequently to different foster homes. From the DHS records, you learn that many different therapists and caseworkers have been assigned to Rodrigo's case. There are literally several hundred pages of records that the attorneys ask you to review, cross-reference, and summarize for an expert in developmental psychology.

Rodrigo is facing first-degree murder charges in adult court. A reverse-transfer hearing is scheduled in 8 months. The lead attorney wants you to review the lengthy discovery (police reports, witness interviews, etc.) about the alleged incident. In addition to summarizing the records for the expert, the defense team would like you to provide emotional support to Rodrigo while he remains in a juvenile detention facility.

In speaking with Rodrigo, he describes issues with bullying, which he says led him to carry a gun "to protect myself." Rodrigo continues to express grief over the "loss" of his brother at a young age and wants you to find him. You eventually learn that one of Rodrigo's first foster families was neglectful and abusive. Rodrigo has a close connection with his most recent foster mother, who tries her best to visit him monthly. His biological family is from a rural area of Mexico, and several family members who live near where Rodrigo is being detained are Spanish-speaking only.

Rodrigo's defense team wants the forensic social worker to support Rodrigo during this process of court proceedings in adult court as a juvenile and to interview all of his biological family members and his foster family. Furthermore, the attorneys want the forensic social worker to build a mitigation packet in time for the reverse-transfer hearing to assist in keeping Rodrigo's cases in juvenile court. If/when this goal is met, the defense team will want the social worker to expand upon the mitigation packet to address alternative placement and treatment options to the court.

Case Study #4 (Jamie)

Jamie is a 14-year-old individual who has no juvenile record and is entering the juvenile court system on charges of trespassing, burglary, and vandalism of her friend Christa's house. Christa is also her codefendant as the two girls allegedly planned to break into Christa's mother's house together. The two girls had not known each other long, and Jamie insists that she did not know that Christa was going to burglarize her own home. Jamie is a freshman in high school and struggling with her identity and bullying at school. Jamie was born as a biological male but has always identified as a female. She recently made the choice to "come out" to her friends and family, and wants to be referred to using the pronoun "she."

The criminal defense-based social worker meets Jamie at the youth detention center. The social worker is surprised that Jamie is still detained because she has no previous system involvement and is not charged with a crime of violence. Jamie reveals to the social worker that she does not have a good relationship with her parents right now. Jamie states that her parents are divorced, and they are "barely talking to me" because Jamie recently told them that she identifies as a female and would like to be called "she." The social worker concludes that leading up to Jamie's arrest, she was experiencing difficult life changes and has struggled with the lack of support from family and former friends. Jamie also reports that staff at the detention facility are discriminating against her because of her identifying as a woman. They are making insensitive comments and continuing to refer to Jamie as a "he." Moreover, the facility's policy states that because of her anatomy, Jamie must be housed with the adolescent boys, which is causing her distress.

The criminal defense-based social worker will be tasked with obtaining Jamie's life history and better assessing what stressful life events may have led up to the alleged crime, interviewing family members and friends, and helping to advocate for Jamie at the detention facility. The social worker is asked to assess whether Jamie should be released on bond and returned to the home of either parent, including whether either parent's home is safer than the detention facility, taking into account that Jamie may not be welcome based on her parents' disapproval of her choice to identify as a woman and the discrimination occurring at the facility.

Appendix 1.1

A DEVELOPMENTAL FRAMEWORK FOR JUVENILE CASES

ROPER/GRAHAM/MILLER	DEVELOPMENT	OFFENSE	POLICE QUESTIONING	SERVICES
• Behavioral immaturity mirrors brain anatomical immaturity	**IMMATURITY**			*Must be tailored to each youth's unique needs, but could*
• Frontal lobe-responsible for impulse control, judgment,	• ***Immature thinking***		"It was a mistake.It was an accident."	*include services (in a facility or the community) such as*:
decision-making-develops slowly until early 20's	-Unable to anticipate	Did not plan: "it happened." Impulsive	Can't look ahead to statement in court	Instruction in anticipating consequences
• Rely on amygdala, primitive emotion center of brain when	-Unable to see choices	Had weapon with no plan to use	"Only way to go home is say what they want"	Instruction in how to see choices & pros & cons
adults process similar information through frontal cortex	-Minimizes risk	No danger in street activities, getting high	"Can always take back what I said"	Instruction in decision-making: think before acting
		"It's just talk." Sexting/social media=harmless	Can't see magnitude of situation	Learning how to manage stress
• Prone to risk-taking; it is statistically aberrant to refrain	• ***Immature identity***			Being successful at something & opportunities to show it
from risk-taking in adolescence	-Not successful	Sensitive to being picked on. Bullied	Self-conscious about being "slow"	Guided process for defining self; becoming a leader
	-Unstable self-definition	Does not ask for adult help	Unsure of self; hurt if called a liar	Instruction in how to think without being influenced
• More susceptible to stress, which further distorts already	-Wants acceptance	Wants to belong even with negative peers	Compliant; does what is asked	Improved social skills to be acceptable to positive peers
poor cost-benefit analysis	-Can't function independently	Needs supervision. Influenced by older codf	Naively trusts police; taught to tell truth	Preparation for work, given talents and disabilities
				Developing job skills; support on the job for good decisions
• Most adolescent delinquent behavior occurs on a social	• ***Moral development***	May have been righting a wrong	Can't believe police would manpulate, lie	Learning positive ways to deal with unfairness
stage where immediate pressure of peers is the real motive	-Fairness fanatic	Did not realize there would be a victim	Snitching=morally wrong	Practicing good moral reasoning under stress
• More vulnerable to peer pressure. Importance of approval	-Empathy	Under stress,can't use usual moral beliefs	Does not understand rights	Victim empathy awareness
makes already risk-prone impulsive teen even more so	-Fragile moral reasoning	Can't walk away, especially when high,	In shock about offense; shame	Specialized instruction to:
		even though knows right from wrong	Believes police will help	• Improve reading by learning how to decode words
• Trauma makes youth hypervigilant in response to threat				• Improve comprehension
	DISABILITIES			• Improve self-talk & communication skills
• Character is not fully formed, and adolescents' signature qualities	• ***Processing problems***	Can't comprehend others' intentions	Doesn't comprehend meaning of Miranda	• Improve sequencing: seeing cause & effect
–including their susceptibility to peer influence and weaknesses	(digesting information)	"Things happened too fast"	Can't follow questions-doesn't ask	• Practicing comprehending instructions
in self-regulation–reflect their incomplete identity	• ***Expressive/receptive language***	Poor communication. Stories out of order.	Difficulty explaining self;confused narrative	• Improve organization; learn how to prioritize
	• ***Executive function deficits***	Poor planner; organizing difficulties	Focuses on getting it over with	• Learn how to concentrate & manage distractibility
• Normal adolescents cannot be expected to operate w/ maturity,	• ***Impaired sequencing***	Couldn't envision what would happen next	Thinking compromised by lack of sleep,	Trauma treatment to:
judgment, risk aversion or impulse control of an adult; teen	• ***Difficulty concentrating***	Became agitated under stress	cold, hunger, other conditions	• Help in writing complete trauma history
who has suffered brain trauma, dysfunctional family, abuse				• See connections between triggers, feelings, & actions
or violence cannot operate at standard levels for adolescents				& learn to respond differently
	TRAUMA (causes delayed development)			• Separate past maltreatment from present provocations
• The vast majority of adolescents who engage in delinquent	• ***Over-reacts to threat***	If victim aggressive, responds as if a repeat	Scared of police, especially 2-on-1	• Learning not to blame self; stop self-destructive acts
behavior desist from crime as they mature		of past maltreatment (reflex reaction)	Easily pressured by overwhelming evidence	• Not assume others are hostile; not act like a victim
• Even the highest risk youths can be rehabilitated effectively	• ***High anxiety***	Controlling. Reacts to change. Can't soothe self	Tearful, exhausted, little eye contact; slow	Learning emotional regulation; label & express feelings
• Youth crime participation may be necessary to avoid threat	• ***Depressed***	Emotion regulation problems Self-harming	thinking; gives in easily; overwhelmed	Learning to anticipate loss of control & how to manage
• Adolescents are far less able than adults to assist their counsel	• ***Numbs feelings with***	Lowered inhibitions, poor judgment if	High, coming down during questioning	Learning to soothe self when agitated without substances
or make important legal decisions	***substances***	high during offense		Help with family where there is conflict or substance abuse

References

American Medical Association. (2005). Amici curiae brief supporting respondent *Roper v. Simmons*. 543 U.S. 551 No. 03–633, 4–20.

American Psychological Association. (2012). Amici curiae brief in support of petitioners, *Miller v. Alabama*. 567 U.S. 460 No. 10–9646, 19–20.

Andrews, A.B. (1991). Social work expert testimony regarding mitigation in capital sentencing proceedings. *Social Work*, *36*, 440–445.

Beyer, M. (2011). A developmental view of youth in the juvenile justice system. In F. Sherman & F. Jacobs (Eds.), *Juvenile justice: Advancing research, policy, and practice*. Hoboken, NJ: Wiley.

Buchanan, S., & Nooe, R.M. (2017). Defining social work within holistic public defense: Challenges and implications for practice. *Social Work, 62*(4), 33–339. doi:10.1093/sw/swx032

Graham v. Florida, 560 U.S. 48 (2010).

Guin, C.C., Noble, D., Merrill, T.S. (2003). From misery to mission: Forensic social workers on multidisciplinary mitigation teams. *Social Work, 48*(3), 362–370.

Miller, J. (September/October 1995). Expanding the spheres of mitigation evidence. *Capital Report 44*, 2–6.

Miller v. Alabama. 567 U.S. 460 (2012).

Roper v. Simmons. 543 U.S. 551 (2005).

Schroeder, J.C. (2003). Social work's role in death penalty mitigation investigations: Forging a new practice area. *Families in Society*, *84*, 423–432.

Steinberg, L. (2014). *Age of opportunity: Lessons from the new science of adolescence*. Boston, MA: Houghton Mifflin Harcourt.

Stevenson, B. (2014). *Just mercy*. New York, NY: Spiegel and Grau.

2

GUIDING PRINCIPLES OF PRACTICE

A Critical Interdisciplinary Approach Toward Effective Client Representation and Advocacy

Ashley Ratliff, Maren Willins, and Sarah Buchanan

Abstract

This chapter will briefly explore the roles that social workers have traditionally played in criminal justice field and discuss the evolving role of forensic social workers in an ever-evolving field of practice. The commonalities between legal ethics and social work ethics will be presented, followed by areas of potential ethical differences between the two professions. Lastly, case examples will convey some ethical concerns that can arise with clients. The case studies will also exemplify how to anticipate and resolve ethical dilemmas based on the employee model.

Learning Objectives

- Understand how social work has played a role, historically, in combating the consequences of poverty and social injustice within the criminal and juvenile justice systems
- Understand legal frameworks which guided this model of criminal defense-based forensic social work
- Understand the attorney-client privilege and how it relates to forensic social workers on the defense team within the employee model of practice
- Begin the discussion of ethical standards and considerations within the growing arena of criminal defense-based forensic social work.

The inception of social work as a profession was rooted in helping impoverished, oppressed, and vulnerable populations in our communities and this chapter explores the ever-evolving role of a forensic social worker. From its historic roots to modern-day standards, the role of a social worker working with clients facing criminal court prosecution or having been sentenced for a criminal conviction or adjudication is a critical aspect of comprehensive client-centered holistic representation in any case. This chapter will take a look at existing standards of practice and legal frameworks for a few identified areas of criminal defense practice as well as provide an overview of the ethical guidelines in place for attorneys which extend to their agents—forensic social workers on criminal defense teams are agents of the attorney under an employee model of practice. While forensic social workers have been involved in juvenile and criminal justice for decades, that role has historically been in assessment, treatment, community supervision, that is, parole and probation as well as victim advocacy. However, the knowledge, skills, and ethics of social work have always aligned with the needs of those in the criminal court systems. While some traditional roles of a forensic social worker may have historically been from a more punitive angle, the unique skills and roles that social workers have guided the practice, and certainly lend themselves toward advocacy, rehabilitative outcomes, and a community supportive outcome versus purely punitive sanctions from criminal behavior. After reviewing some key legal foundations, principles, and guidelines, a couple of fictional client case studies will be explored to convey some of the critical aspects of these guiding principles of practice.

Historical Foundations

Concern about the consequences of poverty and social injustice has been a hallmark of the social work profession from its early roots in the early 19th century, with "friendly visitors" and organizations such as the Association for the Improvement of the Condition of the Poor, to today's mission "to enhance human well-being and help meet the basic human needs of all people, with particular attention to the needs and empowerment of people who are vulnerable, oppressed, and living in poverty" (NASW, 2018). Attention to the legal rights of indigent individuals by the criminal justice system, however, has lagged. A landmark Supreme Court ruling—*Gideon v. Wainwright*—prompted the systematic creation of public defense systems to serve indigent individuals, but that didn't happen until 1963. The Sixth Amendment of the United States Constitution guarantees the right to counsel, but it wasn't until *Gideon* that counsel was guaranteed at no cost for indigent individuals charged with felony crimes. Four years later, the United States Supreme Court secured the right to counsel for juvenile defendants (*In Re Gault*, 1967). Also, during this time, the Court reiterated the importance in providing effective assistance of counsel, especially where a juvenile is facing adult prosecution and life in prison (*Kent v. United States*, 1966). By 1972, the Supreme Court further extended the right to include any crime punishable by imprisonment. For a closer look at historical and guiding influences of forensic social work, see Appendix 2.1, Time Line of History in Forensic Social Work.

Social workers have been working to develop effective and socially just alternatives to incarceration in public defender systems across the country for several decades with "few guideposts or models" (Hisle, Shdaimah & Finegar, 2012; Senna, 1975; Wald, 1972). Opportunities for social workers within this system have expanded and evolved, and social workers have increasingly been integrated as members of defense teams and providing the profession with a tremendous opportunity to serve a population with which the profession has long claimed allegiance (Buchanan & Nooe, 2017). In fact, the guiding principles outlined by the National Association for Public Defense (2018) state that effective public defense depends, in part, on social workers being part of the defense team.

Because this partnership between attorneys and social workers is so critical to best represent the most vulnerable populations—juveniles, young adults, and others charged with crimes in the juvenile and criminal court systems—it was important not only to review existing standards of practice but also to consult with mitigation specialists and forensic social workers in states where social workers were working with the defense teams on staff. The authors of this book set out to create a model of holistic defense to ensure effective assistance of counsel to the most vulnerable clients, which is best implemented through the inclusion of a forensic social worker on criminal defense team. In order to implement this model and work toward its expansion to any client's case, the authors individually and collectively sought out extensive training by defenders and social workers already employing a holistic or interdisciplinary model of criminal defense. In doing so, the practitioners here conducted in-depth research and engaged in numerous trainings with expert attorneys, mitigation specialists, and social workers involved in capital cases.

This model of practice was new to Colorado 5 years ago. In order to best introduce social workers into criminal defense teams, extensive training was provided to attorneys appointed as counsel for indigent defendants, members of the private defense bar, and social workers who would become part of these teams. At the outset, training for social workers has included basic information related to criminal defense, specialized practice areas related to youth in juvenile and adult criminal courts, and the intersection of ethical standards in the legal and social work fields. This includes the role of the social worker as an agent of the attorney, issues related to attorney-client privilege, and the impact of mandatory reporting laws on client confidentiality. Simultaneously, attorneys received training related to the roles and skills bring to the table in best representation of a client. Additionally, training for both attorneys and social workers has included team dynamics, mitigation investigation, the presentation of mitigation stories, and working as a team for the benefit of a client. Over the years, the practitioners at the heart of this book have taken large steps to receive training, present at trainings locally and nationally as well as continue to engage in ongoing education to become experts in this interdisciplinary practice and the lessons learned are provided throughout this book.

Standards of Practice

A criminal defense attorney will refer to local or national standards of practice as a starting place when representing any person charged with a crime. The following sections will include some specific guidelines that have been promulgated in specialized areas of criminal defense practice. The following sample standards of practice are those which primarily guided the inception of the Colorado Model of Criminal Defense-Based Social Work. While these standards may be particular to specific areas of practice, application can be generalized to any person accused of a crime in a client-centered and a holistic manner.

Juvenile Defense Standards—Representation of Children in Juvenile and Adult Criminal Courts

Juvenile defense is a complex and specialized field requiring unique expertise and skills. This includes not only a thorough understanding of the laws impacting juveniles but also knowledge of adolescent and developmental psychology, and engagement with clients' educational, mental health, housing, and familial relationship goals. Effective juvenile defense requires interdisciplinary teams, and a forensic social worker breathes life into the constitutional jurisprudence of effective assistance of counsel. In 2012, the National Juvenile Defender Center (NJDC) promulgated standards of practice now widely accepted by many practitioners. The NJDC asserts, and practitioners agree, that juvenile attorneys have an ethical obligation to develop an awareness of the strengths and needs of their client, the client's family and community, and other social structures; an understanding of child and adolescent development to effectively communicate with clients and evaluate their clients' level of maturity and competency; knowledge of and contacts at community-based programs to compose individualized disposition plans; familiarity with mental health, education, special education, and immigration laws and services; the ability to enlist the child's parent or guardian as an ally without compromising the attorney-client relationship; and the ability to help clients understand the direct and collateral consequences of their decisions (NJDC, 2012).

Traditional legal education does not ordinarily provide the specialized and unique skills required for juvenile defenders; however, many experts in the field of juvenile defense and NJDC provide education and training to the legal profession consistent with the National Juvenile Defense Standards. Recently, Colorado developed a juvenile defense manual to provide practitioners with the vast research and authority to best meet the needs of Colorado's youth in the court system (Colorado Office of Alternate Defense Counsel & Colorado Juvenile Defender Center, 2018). Many states may have their own manual or practice standards for best representation of youth; those mentioned here are just a sample. Meanwhile, social workers receive extensive training in the important facets of understanding and advocating for youth in the criminal court system—their inclusion on defense teams is not only logical but also critical toward best representation of youth.

Representation of Youth at Risk of Adult Court Prosecution

The prosecution of children in adult courts generally replaces the long-standing developmentally based rehabilitation principles inherent to juvenile court with much more severe punishment under adult sentencing schemes. While the configuration of each state's statutory scheme for trying children as adults varies, the statues are commonly grouped into the following categories:

> <u>Discretionary "judicial waiver" or "judicial transfer" statutes</u>: These statutes provide concurrent jurisdiction between juvenile and criminal courts by granting juvenile court judges the discretion to decide whether a juvenile's case should be transferred from juvenile court to adult/criminal court; [note reverse waiver/transfer?]
>
> <u>"Statutory exclusion" or "automatic waiver" or "mandatory waiver" statutes</u>: These statutes exclude certain crimes from the jurisdiction of the juvenile court by requiring the designated crimes be filed only in adult criminal court; and
>
> <u>"Direct file" statutes</u>: These statutes provide for concurrent jurisdiction between the juvenile and criminal courts by giving prosecutors the power to decide whether charges should be filed in juvenile or adult court.

Each method allocates to different branches of government—judicial, legislative, and executive—the decision of whether to prosecute youth under 18 as juveniles or adults (Griffin, Addie, Adams & Firestine, 2011). In Colorado, a juvenile can be prosecuted in adult court by way of judicial transfer or through direct file, but the principles of criminal defense-based forensic social work in this book apply in any jurisdiction regardless of how juveniles enter adult court.

Under the judicial transfer statute, a prosecutor may file a delinquency petition in juvenile court requesting a transfer to adult court, but discretion lies with the juvenile court judge who decides whether to retain or waive jurisdiction. Under the Colorado direct file statute, the prosecutor may directly file a criminal complaint in adult court if certain statutory factors exist for any juvenile who is 16 years or older and charged with specified crimes. In 2012, the Colorado legislature amended its statute, authorizing this direct file procedure to allow a juvenile to request a hearing to transfer the case back to juvenile court (referred to in the statute as a "reverse-transfer" proceeding) (Colorado Revised Statue Sec. 19-2-517 (2012)). This reverse-transfer proceeding provides factors for the court to consider at a hearing on jurisdiction. The statutory factors in Colorado, which many states have adopted in some fashion within their judicial waiver or transfer mechanisms, are based in part around those offered within the United State Supreme Court

Opinion, *Kent v. United States* (*Kent v. U.S.*, 1966). There the Court held that a juvenile is entitled to counsel and due process protections at waiver or transfer hearings. The following are a list of factors that are similar to those in statutory schemes throughout the United States where juveniles are prosecuted as adults.

> The determinative factors which will be considered by the Judge in deciding whether the Juvenile Court's jurisdiction over such offenses will be waived are the following:
>
> 1. The seriousness of the alleged offense to the community and whether the protection of the community requires waiver.
> 2. Whether the alleged offense was committed in an aggressive, violent, premeditated or willful manner.
> 3. Whether the alleged offense was against persons or against property, greater weight being given to offenses against persons especially if personal injury resulted.
> 4. The prosecutive merit of the complaint, i.e., whether there is evidence upon which a Grand Jury may be expected to return an indictment (to be determined by consultation with the United States Attorney).
> 5. The desirability of trial and disposition of the entire offense in one court when the juvenile's associates in the alleged offense are adults who will be charged with a crime in the U.S. District Court for the District of Columbia.
> 6. The sophistication and maturity of the juvenile as determined by consideration of his home, environmental situation, emotional attitude and pattern of living.
> 7. The record and previous history of the juvenile, including previous contacts with the Youth Aid Division, other law enforcement agencies, juvenile courts and other jurisdictions, prior periods of probation to this Court, or prior commitments to juvenile institutions.
> 8. The prospects for adequate protection of the public and the likelihood of reasonable rehabilitation of the juvenile (if he is found to have committed the alleged offense) by the use of procedures, services and facilities currently available to the Juvenile Court.
>
> *(Kent v. United States, 1966)*

These factors provide a skeleton with which a defense team must dig deep into a client's life story in order to find the evidence necessary to inform the court when making an important decision of which jurisdiction a juvenile's case will be prosecuted. Juvenile and adult sentencing schemes are drastically different—one more rehabilitative in nature and the other more punitive, and in most states mandatory prison terms are common. A forensic social worker with background and training in ecological systems (person-in-environment) theory, together with a trauma-informed approach, is the professional on a team who can best assist in telling the client's story and to assist the defense team toward a robust presentation in a developmental manner to any decision-maker.

Representation of children facing adult prosecution as well as young men and women serving unconstitutional sentences is an even more unique and specialized area of practice that led the authors to design this model of criminal defense-based forensic social work. This area of criminal defense was just beginning to develop standards of practice in the wake of the seminal United States Supreme Court cases impacting juvenile sentencing after the infusion of developmental science into the law (CFSY, 2015). Practitioners and experts across the country came together to create standards of practice for those working with youth facing life sentences and applicable to juvenile life without parole resentencing cases, based in part upon the American Bar Association's guidelines for Capitol Defense and Mitigation as well as standards in place for juvenile defense (CFSY, 2015). These practice guidelines were created as a means to help practitioners best implement the mandates of the recent constitutional jurisprudence in the area of juvenile sentencing. Specifically, when the Court held that in order to sentence a juvenile convicted as an adult of first-degree murder to life in prison, a trial court must make individualized findings about an appropriate sentence, the Court specified a list of factors that must be considered (*Miller v. Alabama*, 2012). The Court later affirmed more clearly that the imposition of life in prison upon a juvenile, must be only for the rare offender whose crime does not reflect transient immaturity associated with youth (*Montgomery v. Louisiana*, 2016). The *Miller* factors include (1) the juvenile's "chronological age" and related "immaturity, impetuosity, and failure to appreciate risks and consequences"; (2) the juvenile's "family and home environment that surrounds him"; (3) "the circumstances of the homicide offense, including the extent of his participation in the conduct and the way familial and peer pressures may have affected him"; (4) the "incompetencies associated with youth" in dealing with law enforcement and a criminal justice system designed for adults; and (5) "the possibility of rehabilitation" (*Miller v. Alabama*, 2012). These factors also provide a framework and starting place for any practitioner seeking to present a developmental picture of a client. The aforementioned factors included in legal case law or statutory provisions lend themselves to in-depth mitigation investigation and can be implemented when working on any criminal defense case. A forensic social worker is an invaluable member of the defense team to best help accomplish the important goal of reaching developmentally sound justice.

Ethical Considerations—The Attorney-Client Relationship

Once a person is charged with a crime, an attorney is either appointed by the Court or hired privately by the client to represent that individual. The attorney is the lead of the defense team, which often includes an investigator and a paralegal and today more often than not, a forensic social worker. Ethical rules govern the practice of law and, in turn, the lawyer's agents, which often include investigators and administrative personnel. A social worker on a criminal defense team becomes an agent of the attorney and, as such, must adhere to the rules of professional conduct governing attorneys (Andrews, 2012).

While there are numerous commonalities between the ethics attorneys adhere to and those of a social worker in general, there may be some places or jurisdictions where the two fields may conflict or where tension between the two professions may arise. This section will provide an overview of the ethical guidelines for attorneys promulgated by the American Bar Association (ABA) which have been adopted in some form or capacity in every state as well as a sampling of case law governing the attorney-client relationship, privilege, and confidentiality.

Attorney-Client Privilege and Confidentiality—Communications

Attorneys are bound by rules governing professional conduct. The ABA has developed model rules, but each state will have some form of similar rules of its own. The ethical rule requiring that all communications between an attorney and his or her client be confident is at the heart of the attorney-client relationship. A client must have absolute confidence that his attorney will maintain this confidential relationship, or the client will not confide matters of great importance for effective representation. Further, the bedrock of confidential communications insures effective assistance of counsel, which required by the United States Constitution.

Attorneys "shall not reveal information relating to representation, unless the client gives informed consent, or the disclosure is implicit" (Colorado Rules of Professional Conduct Rule 1.6 (a) Confidentiality of Information, 2018). The attorney's ethical obligations are to keep confidential any and all information related to the representation to the client. This can include the basic fact that the lawyer is even representing an individual. Some jurisdictions provide some limited circumstances in which an attorney *may* disclose information (Colorado Rules of Professional Conduct Rule 1.6 (b) Confidentiality of Information, 2018). But even in jurisdictions which allow some limited disclosures, there typically is no mandatory disclosure requirement in order to ensure protection of the attorney-client relationship and confidential communications.

This important and critical aspect of the attorney-client relationship extends to all agents of the attorney, which includes investigators, paralegals, administrative staff, and also forensic social workers working with a client under the supervision and direction of an attorney. In addition, the duty to confidentiality has been extended to other agents, including expert witnesses acting on behalf of the lawyer, as long as the purpose of the communication is the securing of information to render legal advice" (*B.B. v. People*, Colo. 1990; *People v. Johnson*, Colo. 2000). Thus, statements made by a client to a lawyer's agents, including a forensic social worker on a criminal defense team, are under the umbrella of the attorney's representation and within the scope of the attorney's representation of the client.

Lawyers who employ or retain nonlawyer assistants are required to "make reasonable efforts to ensure that the person's conduct is compatible with the professional obligations of the lawyer" (American Bar Association, Rule 5.3, 2013). Furthermore, unless otherwise stated or pursuant to local statutes, "[t]he lawyer's obligation of confidentiality takes precedence over any obligation of disclosure that is imposed upon social workers or other health care professionals when they are working for the lawyer on any matter" (NAPD, 2014). Each state will have its own rules and laws related to the attorney-client relationship and the obligations of agents. Some states have carved out exceptions to mandated reporting requirements for social workers working as part of a defense team. It is important that any practitioner—social worker or attorney—understands the governing rules in their jurisdiction. For an initial look at state-by-state mandatory reporting for attorneys or social workers, see Appendix 2.2; *The Interdisciplinary Defense Team & Confidentiality: What Defenders Need to Know* (2016) 50—State Survey of Child Abuse Mandatory Reporting Statutes (NLADA, 2016). In Colorado, the attorney-client privilege includes forensic social workers working on defense teams as part of the representation of an accused juvenile or adult. Social workers are considered agents of the attorney and have the same obligations of confidentiality and privileged communications when working with clients in this unique capacity.

Attorney-Client Privilege and Confidentiality—Work Product

The attorney-client privilege also protects the contents of a defense attorney's case file. Similar to the importance of confidential communications, protection of an attorney's work product was developed to promote frank discussions between a lawyer and his or her client, along with the ability to fully explore the best means of representing a client which may not otherwise occur absent the protection (*People v. Madera*, 2005). The attorney-client privilege applies to "confidential matters communicated by or to the client in the course of obtaining counsel, advice, or direction with respect to the client's rights or obligations" (*People v. Madera*, Colo. 2005). This privilege is personal with the client and can only be waived by the client *(Losavio v. Dist. Court*, Colo. 1975).

In Colorado, courts have distinguished between "factual" and "opinion" work product *(People v. Angel* Colo. 2012) (Bergman & Hollander, 2011). As stated by Bergman and Hollander and cited in *People v. Angel, supra,*

> [g]enerally, '[o]pinion work product includes the attorney's mental impressions, opinions or legal theories' and is afforded a high level of protection. In contrast, factual work product encompasses the factual observations memorialized by an attorney while conducting an investigation and generally receives a lower level of protection.
>
> (People v. Angel, 2012) *(Bergman & Hollander, 2011).*

A forensic social worker will develop both opinion and factual work product. While the rules vary across jurisdictions and are far more complicated than what can be described in this book, generally, factual work product involves recitations of objective facts and observations, and opinion work product includes mental impressions, such as a client's psychological functioning, potential mental health diagnoses, psychosocial aspects of a client's case or circumstances, as well as concerns about suicide or the like. Factual work product can include written information which detail a social worker's interviews with mitigation witnesses, and certain interactions with a client or other witness that is documented objectively and lacks detail that could be described as an impression, opinion, or recommendation. A forensic social worker produces a variety of more complex work product, such as biopsychosocial assessments, mitigation reports, genograms, time lines, ecomaps, and reentry and sentencing assessments. Depending upon whether these reports contain impressions, recommendations, opinions, or conclusions will generally determine whether the work product is considered factual or opinion. Opinion work product has a greater chance of remaining confidential if the social worker testifies in a fact-witness capacity and not as an expert. The decision about the capacity in which a forensic social worker will testify lies with the attorney.

Under most ethical rules governing the practice of law, both opinion and factual work product would be protected, in most circumstances. However, it is important to note that work product will not and cannot always remain confidential. In instances of a potential waiver, opinion work product will likely, depending on the rules of the specific jurisdiction, receive a higher degree of protection than factual work product. Therefore, it is important for a forensic social worker to understand the distinction between the two.

Waiver of Confidentiality and Privilege

Rules concerning the confidentiality of privileged communications and work product for agents of the attorney, which includes the defense-based forensic social worker, will vary depending on the state or jurisdiction, and it is impossible for this chapter to include every caveat concerning confidentiality and waiver. Suffice to say, however, that any attorney will be concerned about the potential for waiving the confidentiality of what would otherwise be protected. The decision whether to waive a professional privilege rests squarely with the attorney on the case and, ultimately, the client—not the forensic social worker. Therefore, it is important for the forensic social worker to understand the general principles and exercise diligence in maintaining privilege and confidentiality unless or until the attorney authorizes such disclosure. An understanding of these principles will aid the forensic social worker as she develops work product. Attorneys are obligated to ensure that their agents know, understand, and abide by the ethical rules of professional conduct.

There are a number of scenarios in which the attorney could either implicitly or explicitly authorize disclosure of otherwise protected information or work product. One such example is that of providing information to the prosecution for purposes of negotiating a favorable agreed upon resolution to a case (this is often referred to as a "plea bargain"). For a variety of reasons that are beyond the scope of this chapter or book, the vast majority of criminal cases result in a plea bargain. This typically means the person charged enters a plea of guilty in order to receive in exchange a reduced charge or reduced sentence. Attorneys often provide work product to prosecutors in order to aid in the negotiation of a plea bargain, thereby explicitly waiving privilege. This sort of waiver can similarly occur in a situation in which an attorney chooses to provide information to a judge overseeing a hearing or sentencing when the work product developed can aid the judge in deciding a particular issue. For instance, an attorney may choose to provide a report generated by a forensic social worker to a judge in order to obtain a more favorable sentence for the client. Further, work product waiver can occur when strategic decisions concerning a criminal case are made by an attorney, such as when a plea of not guilty by reason of insanity is entered or when an expert is called who relied upon certain information. This is discussed in more detail in Chapter 7, "Forensic Social Work and Collaboration with Expert Witnesses" of this book.

That said, it is important for a forensic social worker to be mindful and aware at all times of the potential for her or his work product to be provided to a third party and should ensure that the attorney on the case specifies adequate direction concerning the development or production of work product. This should be achieved through early and ongoing conversations between the forensic social worker and attorney on each individual case, as well as transparent conversations with the client, about how work product can and will be developed and utilized. Forensic social workers should be particularly mindful of reminding the client that the social worker is a member of the criminal defense team, and thus shares all meaningful client information directly with the attorney and other defense team members. Moreover, the social worker, along with the attorney, should always let the client know when and how much of their information will be shared beyond the legal team; the purpose for the disclosure; and in what format, that is, a biopsychosocial assessment, a time line, or during a mitigation meeting with the district attorneys prosecuting the client's case, it may ultimately be disclosed to any number of outside third parties, and it is important for the client to be aware of this possibility and reminded that this decision is up to the attorney and, ultimately, the client.

The importance of recognizing a potential waiver of privilege is especially important in capital or death penalty cases where there may be increased disclosure requirements. For instance, in Colorado, as in most states where the death penalty is a possible penalty, rules exist which require an attorney to disclose not only the subject matter of a witness's testimony but also any written or recorded statements of that witness, including notes that relate to the subject matter of the testimony (Colorado Rules of Criminal Procedure 32-1(d)(7)(A)(I)). It is very important that the forensic social worker and the attorney discuss early on whether the forensic social worker might testify as that role clarification will help the social worker know what work product he or she will produce for her own assessment process or to help inform other team members.

Ethical Considerations—Social Worker as an Agent of the Defense Team

As previously mentioned, forensic social work dates back to social work's roots in juvenile and social justice. Today, criminal defense-based social work continues to be an evolving field and practice. The ethical principles that guide and define the field of forensic social work will continue to evolve on the national, state, and agency levels. At the time of this writing, ethical principles are not consistent from state to state. Since this book focuses on the employee model of practice, ethical standards will apply to this model.

The NASW states that the national Code of Social Work Ethics include the following values of social work (NASW, 2018):

- Service
- Social justice
- Dignity and worth of the person
- Importance of human relationships
- Integrity
- Competence.

The NASW states that the Ethical Standards include (NASW, 2018):

- Commitment to clients
- Self-determination
- Informed consent
- Competence
- Cultural awareness & social diversity
- Conflicts of interest
- Privacy & confidentiality
- Access to records
- No sexual relationships
- No physical contact
- No sexual harassment
- Derogatory language
- Payment for services
- Others related to a client's competence, interruption of services, and referral and termination.

A social worker working in a forensic social work role can and should maintain the National Association of Social Work's values and ethics outlined earlier. However, there are times when a social worker's ethical guidelines may not align with the ethics outlined for attorneys. For example, in all states, social workers are considered mandatory reporters. However, whether or not a social worker on a criminal defense team is considered a mandatory reporter varies from state to state. Knowing the individual state requirements is key to criminal defense-based forensic social work (see Appendix 2.2, *The Interdisciplinary Defense Team & Confidentiality: What Defenders Need to Know* (2016) 50—State Survey of Child Abuse Mandatory Reporting Statutes (NLADA, 2016, reprinted with permission)). Several states, including Colorado, work from an employee model of practice. According to the employee model of practice and the ABA, lawyers that employ or retain nonlawyer assistants are required to "make reasonable efforts to ensure that the person's conduct is compatible with the professional obligations of the lawyer" (ABA, 2013).

Lastly, the agency with whom the forensic social worker is employed or contracted may have its own guidelines and ethical standards for a social worker on a criminal defense team. Following the employee model, the forensic social worker adheres to the same confidentiality requirements as the attorney. While some social workers may struggle with this concept, attorney-client privilege and confidentiality are the cornerstones of criminal defense work. They preserve the dignity of the accused and allow for defense teams and the profession as a whole to remain proficient in defending their clients.

In essence, forensic social workers who are an employee of an attorney representing a client in criminal court are not providing therapy, although they may from time to time employ therapeutic techniques. While defense-based social workers are protected agents of the attorney, a reporting process takes place within the defense team to provide support and services for the client. When a client presents with concerning information, such as thoughts or actions of suicidal ideation, the social worker will report this to the attorney, and together they will process the situation so as to best help the client without compromising the client's protected rights to confidential communications with his or her lawyer and agents. Often, after this initial reporting to the lead attorney, the social worker will be tasked with employing crisis intervention skills and safety planning, among other therapeutic skills or interventions with the client, in close partnership with the attorney. This process is important not only to provide skills for the client in crisis or exhibiting concerning behavior or signs of stress but also to ensure that the reporting is done in a manner that does not cause harm to the client facing criminal charges.

Strategy for Ethical Dilemmas

Like all social work, ethical dilemmas will occur through the course of this work. It can be naïve and dangerous to not be prepared. A preventative and collaborative approach is critical. The social worker and attorney must recognize that ethical issues occur, understand the laws and guidelines related to reporting and the possible tension between legal and social work practice, and clarify the roles and duties of the professionals on the team before they occur, as well as understand that the attorney will make the determination about how to resolve an ethical issue. If the forensic social worker is receiving outside supervision for purposes of licensure or for any other reason, she might also utilize this resource when an ethical dilemma presents.

Case Discussion

To better illustrate, let's revisit the case study of Ben:

During a third visit with Ben, he tells his social worker that he wants to "give up and sleep away." The social worker recognizes this as possible suicidal ideations. The forensic social worker asks Ben to explain more about what he means by giving up and sleeping away? He tells his social worker that he doesn't want to stay in juvenile detention anymore, wishes he could give up on his case and "take a bunch of pills to sleep and not wake up." The social worker uses his/her crisis intervention skills to further assess Ben's intention of suicide to determine that he is thinking of it as an alternative but has no immediate plans. The forensic social worker also determines that Ben does not have the means to act upon his suicidal ideations while at the detention center. Lastly, the forensic social worker guides Ben to write down a safety plan, including how he is going to take care of himself should he continue to have these suicidal ideations. Ben talks about how he "just wants someone to talk to." That becomes the focus of the safety plan—listing whom he can talk with in order including his family members, his social worker, his attorney, the investigator, his one friend at the detention center, and his case manager at the facility. Both sign the safety plan and the social worker explains to Ben that the information will be relayed to the attorney. The attorney is planning to visit the following day, as previously scheduled, and Ben promises to not harm himself until he sees the attorney. If he has those feelings when meeting the attorney, he will tell the attorney. The social worker leaves the facility determining that Ben is in a more stable headspace but that assessing for suicidal ideations will need to happen each visit. The forensic social worker plans to return to visit in 2 days.

Upon the social worker leaving the facility, he/she believes there may be an ethical dilemma in that the attorney will not want Ben to discuss his current situation with his family, who are largely unavailable, or anyone within the facility. The forensic social worker immediately calls the attorney after exiting the detention facility to inform her about what occurred and safety concerns. They are both able to agree that each plus the investigator will visit Ben the next several days to assess any risk. A safety plan will be rewritten to exclude Ben talking with any family other than his one supportive, stable, adult cousin and anyone within the facility. The social worker will assist Ben in filling out a request for a mental health counselor while he is detained whom he may gain therapeutic support from.

Looking to the case study of Jamie, suppose the forensic social worker is concerned about Jamie when visiting her at the detention facility for their second visit. Instead of the usual "fight" and talkativeness in Jamie, the social worker perceives her as being more withdrawn and quieter than she was during their first meeting. Upon asking Jamie more about her shift in demeanor, Jamie responds with "I don't know. I just don't see the point anymore. I have no friends and my parents don't even want me." The forensic social worker is concerned that these may be suicidal ideations and therefore decides to a safety check. The forensic social worker asks Jamie if she is having thoughts of harming herself and she responds "yes." The social worker asks if she has a plan or any means to which Jamie responds, "no they don't let me have anything in here. If I can find something I will cut my wrists."

While the forensic social worker is not concerned about Jamie hurting herself in the immediate future, there is a concern about what Jamie might do if she were to "find something" to use to harm herself. The forensic social worker decides to create a safety plan with Jamie. With some guidance, Jamie can identify that the social worker, her attorney, and a maternal aunt are trusting adults. Jamie and her social worker are able to identify methods to cope with her symptoms of depression, which include suicidal ideation, as journaling about her feelings, reading, doing schoolwork, coloring, walking when the facility allows this, and square-breathing. The forensic social worker tells Jamie that she may call her social worker or attorney as needed, and contracts for safety until one of them is able to visit that afternoon. If Jamie feels like she cannot be safe for a few hours until that visit, she will call one of them immediately.

In a more traditional social work setting, the social worker might be a mandatory reporter if contracting for safety was not a possibility. In this example, the forensic social worker effectively contracts for safety with Jamie and will call the attorney to inform them upon leaving the facility. The forensic social worker and the attorney form a plan to keep Jamie safe by visiting daily; enlisting extra visits and phone calls from the aunt whom Jamie trusts; and encouraging Jamie to talk with the facility's psychiatrist, who has a good reputation and clinical skills with the juvenile facility. While Jamie does not trust the staff at the juvenile facility, she does find the psychiatrist "easy to talk to."

Practical Tips

Even though legal and social work ethics are largely aligned, it would be naïve to ignore that ethical pitfalls might arise. As an agency, it is best to assume that ethical pitfalls will arise so that agency standards can be established. In accordance to the employee model, anticipating potential ethical pitfalls will help to establish these standards. As an agency, a flow of steps should be established that are clear and that consider the legal ethical standards, social work ethical standards and state standards of practice. Generally, protecting client-attorney confidentiality, client safety (i.e., suicidal ideations), mandatory reporting (i.e. reports of abuse and community safety), and client self-determination are the ethical standards that may come into conflict. The following ethical pitfalls explore a flow of steps that might be followed in an employee model criminal defense agency.

Suicidal client

1. Forensic social worker assesses the risk and safety plans with the client directly.
2. When the client is safe enough for the social worker to leave him or her for a bit, call the attorney to inform.
3. If the attorney is unavailable, call and talk with an agency supervisor (preferably a social worker).
4. Organize with the defense team (forensic social worker, attorney, and investigator) to visit and talk with the client as regularly as the client needs until the safety risk is mitigated.
5. If the defense team is not able to help keep the client safe, other options of having a trusted family member (if the client is a juvenile or dependent) or the client (if they are a functioning adult) check into inpatient treatment.

Conclusion

Criminal defense-based forensic social work is a new and evolving field which brings together two professions in a unique collaborative manner toward best representation of clients. The importance of a mitigation investigation for any client is critical. While, historically, mitigation presentation has often been thought of as only essential during capital cases, it is essential that an attorney and their defense team collect and present all mitigation at different points through the life of a case from arrest and possible bond consideration toward plea negotiations, and especially prior to and during sentencing. Mitigation collection that is done properly needs to be rooted in trust and an exhaustive investigation. Finding and developing mitigation themes through interviews and extensive record review helps put together a full psychosocial history of the client. The presentation of mitigation should also craft a persuasive story of the client's life. Within the last few decades, mitigation identification, collection and presentation launching from the model identified in this book, has been more and more utilized in juvenile cases, specifically juvenile life without parole cases or where the juvenile is facing life in prison, and is rapidly becoming the norm in any criminal case for the best defense of a client. By digging deep into our clients' stories, practitioners will inevitably come across or be faced with ethical considerations within the practice. The key to working through any issues that arise and working with clients within the criminal defense-based models of forensic social work is communication. Communication between the professional members of the defense team and a collective understanding of national, state, and agency guiding principles must be continuously revisited and discussed.

Appendix 2.1

Time Line of History in Forensic Social Work

Time Line		
DATE	*Author(s)*	*Purpose*
1963	United States Supreme Court	Unanimously ruled that states are required to provide counsel to indigent defendants
1967	Sloane	Surveyed social workers and lawyers to answer question of how each views the other profession, underlying attitudes; results discuss antagonism/uneasy relationship between professions, remedial approaches offered
1970	Smith	Study explored the relationship between lawyer and social worker in legal aid setting (no criminal work); interviews and attitude scales regarding responsibilities, role perception, and nature of interdisciplinary relationship
1972	Wald	Evaluation of the Offender Rehabilitation Project of the Public Defender Office for Santa Clara County, California
1974	Senna	Social workers in public defender programs; surveyed public defenders and interviewed social workers in public defense settings
1976	Scherrer	How social workers help lawyers; discusses strain and conflict characterizing relationship between the two professions and attempts to answer question of what social work can offer legal profession
1979	Moriarty	Evaluation: Public Defender Social Worker Program, Dade County, FL
1987	Ashford, Macht, & Mylym	Advocacy by social workers in the public defender's office
1990s	Steinberg	Holistic defense model emerges
1999	Galowitz	Collaboration between lawyers and social workers; outlines value in relationship and discussed unique role of social workers; discusses need for social work in public defense
2004	Steinberg & Feige	Cultural revolution: Transforming the public defender's office; social workers as part of holistic model
2004–2015	Texas	Mental Health Public Defender model emerges; 10 offices open across the state; social workers integral to practice in most areas; evaluations occur in most areas (i.e., Travis County, 2016)
2005	Steinberg	How holistic representation makes for good policy, better lawyers, and more satisfied clients

Time Line

DATE	*Author(s)*	*Purpose*
2004–2006	Geurin, Otis & Royse (2013)	Alternative Sentencing Social Worker Field Education Program implemented in KY; students provided alternative sentencing plans; discussed in 2013 paper
2006–2007	Kentucky Department of Public Advocacy (2008)	Social Work Pilot Project implemented; four social workers hired, three evaluated; evaluation report finalized in 2008
2007	Texas	Mental Health Public Defender model of defense emerged in Travis County, TX; social workers integral and work with all clients
2008–2013	Texas	Evaluations of Mental Health Public Defenders underway (social work integral to practice in most areas)
2012	Hisle, Shdaimah & Finegar	Evaluation of Maryland's Holistic Program; social work services evaluated and discussed
2013	Steinberg	Heeding Gideon's Call in the Twenty-First Century: Holistic Defense and the New Public Defense Paradigm; further defines holistic defense and discusses evaluation
2013	Kentucky Department of Public Advocacy	Social Worker Alternative Sentencing Program Pilot Evaluation Study; eight social workers employed by state at this point
2014	Kentucky Department of Public Advocacy (2016)	SFY 2014 Evaluation Report: Kentucky Department of Public Advocacy Alternative Sentencing Worker Program; finalized 2016
2014	Lee, Ostrom & Kleiman	The Measure of Good Lawyering: Evaluating Holistic Defense in Practice; NIJ grant supported work
2014	Davies	How Do We "Do Data" in Public Defense; elaborates on new interest/funding in public defense research
2014	Michigan State Appellate Defender's Office	State Appellate Defender's Office Social Worker Sentencing Program Evaluation
2015	Texas Fair Defense Project/Susanne Pringle	Strengthening Juvenile Defense Representation by Partnering with Social Workers: A Holistic Approach; description of holistic approach and potential impact for juveniles
2016	Kentucky	Social work staff grew from 8 to 45 as a result of evaluation efforts
2016	McCarter Services	Holistic Representation: A Randomized Pilot Study of Wraparound Services

Appendix 2.2

NLADA Chart of Mandatory Reporting by State, *The Interdisciplinary Defense Team & Confidentiality: What Defenders Need to Know* (2016)

The Interdisciplinary Defense Team & Confidentiality: What Defenders Need to Know (2016)
50-State Survey of Child Abuse Mandatory Reporting Statutes

NLADA National Legal Aid & Defender Association nlada.org

State >	Mandatory Reporting Statute	Penalty for Failure to Report	"All Persons" are Reporters	"Social Workers" are Reporters	"Attorneys" are Reporters	Privileges: Recognized & Abrogated	Standard of Knowledge	Notes	State <
AL	Ala. Code §26-14-3	§26-14-13 - MISD. (up to 6 mo. Imprisonment &/or $500 fine)		Yes: §26-14-3(a)	No: §26-14-3(a)	§26-14-10 - attorney-client privilege recognized; §26-14-3(f) - clergy are reporters, clergy-pentitent privilege recognized.	§26-14-3(a) - known or suspected		AL
AK	Alaska Stat. Ann. §47.17.020	§47.17.068 - Class A MISD.		Yes: §47.17.290(14); cross-ref §47.17.020(a)(1)	No: §47.17.020(a)(1)	§47.17.060 - physician-patient and husband-wife privilege abrogated as to evidence of child's harm.	§47.17.020(a) - reasonable cause to suspect; §47.17.290(15) - "reasonable cause to suspect" defined		AK
AZ	A.R.S. §13-3620	§13-3620.O - Class 1 MISD, Class 6 FEL. if failure to report involves a 'reportable offense'		Yes: §13-3620.A.1	No: §13-3620.A.1	§13-3620.A - clergy-penitent privilege recognized.	§13-3620.A - reasonably believes		AZ
AR	A.C.A. §12-18-402	§12-18-201 - Class A MISD.; §12-18-201 - Class C MISD.		Yes: §12-18-402(b)(24)	Yes, for attorneys ad litem: §12-18-402(b)(31)	§12-18-402(c)(1) - privilege shall not prevent reporting if person is mandatory reporter ; §12-18-402(b)(29) - clergy-pentient privilege recognized	§12-18-402(a)(1) - reasonable cause to suspect		AR
CA	Cal Pen Code §11165.7	§11166(c) - MISD. (Up to six months jail &/or $1,000 fine)		Yes: §11165.7(a)(15)	No: §11165.7(a)(1-44)	§11166(d)(1-2) - clergy are reporters, but clergy-pentitent privilege recognized.	§11166(a) - knows or reasonably suspects; §11166(a)(1) "reasonable suspicion" defined	See Elijah W. v. Superior Court, 213 Cal.App.4th 1343 (2013), concluding that "psychotherapist on the defense 'team' ... as experts appointed to aid the defense ... are bound by the attorney-client	CA

State >	Mandatory Reporting Statute	Penalty for Failure to Report	"All Persons" are Reporters	"Social Workers" are Reporters	"Attorneys" are Reporters	Privileges: Recognized & Abrogated	Standard of Knowledge	Notes	State <
CO	C.R.S. §19-3-304	§19-3-304(4) - MISD. & CIVIL liability		Yes: §19-3-304(2)(m)	No: §19-3-304(1)(a-kk)	§19-3-304(2)(aa)(I-III) referencing §13-90-107(1)(c) - clergy are reporters, but clergy-pentitent privilege recognized.	§19-3-304(1)(b)(2) - reasonable cause to know or suspect		CO
CT	Conn. Gen. Stat. §17a-101	§17a-101a(b) - MISD., or FEL. under certain circumstances		Yes: §17a-101(b)(10)	No: §17a-101(b)(1-37)		§17a-101a(a) - reasonable cause to suspect or believe		CT
DE	16 Del. C. §903	§914 - CIVIL, 1st time not to exceed $10,000, from thereon not to exceed $50,000	Yes, "any person, agency, organization or entity": §903	Yes: §903	No: §903	§909 - all privileges abrogated, except attorney-client and clergy-penitent.	§903 - knows or in good faith suspects		DE
DC	D.C. Code §4-1321.02			Yes, with defense team exception: §4-1321.02(b)	No: § 4–1321.02(b)		§4-1321.02(a) - knows or has reasonable cause to suspect	The DC Statute is considered by many to be a model statute, because social workers who are employed by lawyers are specifically exempted from reporting.	DC
FL	Fla. Stat. §39.201	§39.205 - FELONY 3rd Degree (up to 5 years imprisonment &/or $5000 fine)	Yes, "any person": §39.201(1)(a)	Yes: §39.201(1)(d)	No: §39.201(1)(d)	39.204 - all privileges abrogated, except attorney-client and clergy-penitent	§39.201(1)(a-c) - knows, or has reasonable cause to suspect		FL
GA	O.C.G.A. §19-7-5	§19-7-5(h) - MISD.		Yes: §19-7-5(c)(1)(G)	No: §19-7-5(c)(1)(A-O)		§19-7-5(c)(1) - reasonable cause to believe		GA
HI	HRS §350-1.1	§350-1.2 - Petty MISD.		Yes, "individuals… providing social, medical, hospital, or mental health services" : §350-1.1(a)(3)	No: §350-1.1 (a)(1-7)	§350-5 - physician-patient, psychologist-client, spousal, and victim-counselor privilege abrogated. no mention of attorney-client privilege.	§350-1.1(a) - reason to believe		HI

(Continued)

State >	Mandatory Reporting Statute	Penalty for Failure to Report	"All Persons" are Reporters	"Social Workers" are Reporters	"Attorneys" are Reporters	Privileges: Recognized & Abrogated	Standard of Knowledge	Notes	State <
ID	Idaho Code Ann. §16-1605	§16-1605(4) - MISD.	Yes, "any…or other person": §16-1605(1)	Yes: §16-1605(1)	No: §16-1605(1)	§16-1605(3) - clergy-penitent privilege recognized.	§16-1605(1) - reason to believe		ID
IL	325 ILCS 5/4	325 ILCS 5/4.02 - 1st time MISD., from thereon FEL.		Yes: ILCS 5/4		325 ILS 5/4 - attorney-client and clergy-penitent privilege recognized, other professional privileges abrogated.	325 ILS 5/4 - reasonable cause to believe		IL
IN	IC §31-33-5-1	§31-33-22-1 - Class B MISD. (up to 180 days imprisonment &/or $1000 fine)	Yes, "an individual": §31-33-5-1			§31-33-5-1 - various privileges (including social worker) abrogated, attorney-client privilege not mentioned.	§31-33-5-1 - reason to believe		IN
IA	Iowa Code §232.69	§232.75.1- Simple MISD. (up to 30 days imprisonment &/or $65-625 fine); §232.75.2 - CIVIL		Yes: §232.69.1.b(1)	No: §232.69.1.b(1-13)	§232.74 - spousal privilege abrogated, health professional confidentiality abrogated.	§232.69.1.a-b - reasonably believes		IA
KS	K.S.A. §38-2223	§38-2223(e) - Class B MISD. (up to 6 months imprisonment in county jail)		Yes, "licensed social workers": §38-2223(a)(1)(B)	No: §38-2223	§38-2249 - physican/psychologist-patient and social worker-client privileges abrogated	§38-2223(a)(1) - reason to suspect	See Kan. Atty. Gen. Op. No. 01-28, 2001 WL 930603 (2001), concluding that the lawyer should inform both the client and social worker of the social worker's duty to report.	KS
KY	KRS §620.030	§620.030(6) - 1st time, MISD. Class B, 2nd time MISD. Class A, from thereon FEL.	Yes, "any person": §620.030(1)	Yes: §620.030(2)		§620.030(4) - spousal and professional privileges abrogated, attorney-client and clergy-penitent privileges recognized.	§620.030(1) - knows or has reasonable cause to believe		KY

State >	Mandatory Reporting Statute	Penalty for Failure to Report	"All Persons" are Reporters	"Social Workers" are Reporters	"Attorneys" are Reporters	Privileges: Recognized & Abrogated	Standard of Knowledge	Notes	State <
LA	La. Child. Code Ann. Art. 603(17)(a-k), 609	R.S. §14:403 - up to $500 fine &/or 6 months imprisonment; If seriously bodily injury results, up tp $3000 fine &/or 3 years imprisonment		Yes: Art. 603(17)(b)		§14:403.B - all privileges abrogated, except attorney-client and clergy-penitent.	Art. 609 - cause to believe	Social workers are exempted from reporting when engaged by an attorney to represent the child in an abuse case. See Art. 603(17)(b).	LA
ME	22 M.R.S. §4011-A	§4009 - CIVIL (forfeiture up to $500)		Yes: §4011-A.1.A(15)	No: §4011-A.1.A(1-32)	§4015 - spousal and physician/psychotherapist -patient privileges abrogated as to reporting.	§4011-A.1.A - knows or has reasonable cause to suspect	See §4015: "Statements made to a licensed mental health professional in the course of counseling, therapy or evaluation where the privilege is abrogated under this section may not be used against the client in a criminal proceeding."	ME
MD	Md. Family Law Code Ann. §5-702 & 704	§5–705.2(b) - MISD. (up to 5 years imprisonment &/or up to $10,000 fine)		Yes, "human service worker": §5-704	No: §5-704(a)	§5-705(2)(i-iii) - attorney-client privilege and right to counsel recognized; §5-704 - privileges abrogated as to human service workers.	§5-704(a)(1) - reason to believe	See State v. Pratt, 398 A.2d 421 (Md. 1979), concluding that, at least in criminal cases, attorney-client privilege extends to attorney's necessary agents.	MD
MA	ALM GL ch. 119, §51A	§51A(c) - 1st time, up to $2000 fine; 2nd time, fine up to $200 and imprisonment up to 6 months; from thereon, up to $2000 fine and 2.5 years imprisonment		Yes: ch.119, §21		ch.119, §51A(j) - all privileges abrogated, except clergy-penitent.	ch. 119, §51A(a) - reasonable cause to believe		MA
MI	MCLS §722.623	§722.633 - MISD; §722.633 - CIVIL		Yes: §722.623(1)(a)					MI

(Continued)

State >	Mandatory Reporting Statute	Penalty for Failure to Report	"All Persons" are Reporters	"Social Workers" are Reporters	"Attorneys" are Reporters	Privileges: Recognized & Abrogated	Standard of Knowledge	Notes	State <
MN	Minn. Stat. §626.556	§626.556(6)(a) - MISD.		Yes, "social services professional": §626.556.3(a)(1)			§626.556.3(a) - knows or has reason to believe	Under §148E.230.2, a social worker must inform the client of those circumstances under which the social worker may be required to disclose client information.	MN
MS	MS Code. §43-21-353	§43-21-353(4) - MISD.	Yes, "any…or other person": §43-21-353(1)	Yes: §43-21-353(1)	Yes: §43-21-353(1)		§43-21-353 (1) - reasonable cause to suspect		MS
MO	§210.115 R.S.Mo	§210.165 - MISD.		Yes: §210.115.1	No: §210.115.1		§210.115.1 - reasonable cause to suspect		MO
MT	§41-3-201 MCA	§41-3-207(2) - MISD.		Yes: §41-3-201(2)e	No: §41-3-201(2)(a-j)		§41-3-201(1) - knows or has reasonable cause to suspect		MT
NE	R.R.S. Neb. §28-711	§28-717 - MISD.	Yes, "any…or any other person": §28-711(1)	Yes: §28-711(1)	No: §28-711(1)	§28-714. – physician-patient, professional, and spousal privileges abrogated.	§28-711 - reasonable cause to believe		NE
NV	Nev. Rev. Stat. Ann. §202.882; §432B.220.4.	NRS 202.888.2 - MISD.; NRS 432B.240 - MISD.	Yes, "a person": NRS 202.882.1; Exceptions: NRS 202.888.	No: NRS 202.822.; Yes, licensed social worker: NRS 432B.220.4(a)	No: NRS 202.882; Yes: NRS 432B.220(4)(i)	NRS 202.888 - privileges defined in NRS 49.095 recognized, including attorney-client privilege, which extends to attorneys' representatives; NRS 432B.225 - attorney-client privilege recognized	NRS 202.882.1 - knows or has reasonable cause to believe; NRS 432B.220(1) - knows or has reasonable cause to believe	Nevada has two child abuse reporting statutes. §202.882 imposes a duty to report violent or sexual offense against child, whereas § 432B.220.4 imposes a duty to report abuse and neglect. See 2005 State Bar of Nevada's Ethics Committee Formal Opinion No. 30, addressing a previous version of § 432B.220.4, for a discussion of attorney-confidentiality and the statutory duty to report.	NV

State >	Mandatory Reporting Statute	Penalty for Failure to Report	"All Persons" are Reporters	"Social Workers" are Reporters	"Attorneys" are Reporters	Privileges: Recognized & Abrogated	Standard of Knowledge	Notes	State <
NH	N.H. Rev. Stat. Ann. Section 169-C:29	169-C:39 - MISD.	Yes, "any…or any other person": 169-C:29	Yes: 169-C:29	No: 169-C:29	§169-C:32 - spousal and professional-patient/client privileges abrogated, attorney-client privilege recognized.	§169-C:29 - reason to suspect		NH
NJ	N.J. Stat. Ann. §9:6-8.10	§9:6-8.14 - "disorderly person"	Yes, "any person": §9:6-8.10				§9:6-8.10 - reasonable cause to believe		NJ
NM	NMSA §32A-4-3	§32A-4-3.F - MISD.	Yes, "every person": §32A-4-3.A	Yes, social worker acting in an official capacity: NMSA §32A-4-3.A		§32A-4-3.A - clergy-penitent privilege recognized	§32A-4-3.A - knows or has a reasonable suspicion	State v Strauch, 2015-NMSC-009, abrogates the counseling privilege for social workers whose client admits child abuse, since the counseling privilege does not apply where law otherwise requires under NMRA 11-504(D)(4). The New Mexico Supreme Court has not addressed defense team social workers, but attorney-client privilege should ideally be given a broader scope than counseling privilege given the text of NMRA 11-503.B, which explicitly includes representatives of attorneys.	NM
NY	NY CLS Soc Serv §413	§ 420.1 - Class A MISD.; § 420.2 - CIVIL		Yes: §413.1(a)	No: §413.1(a)		§413.1(a) - reasonable cause to suspect child; or parent/caretaker of child tells of personal knowledge of abuse	See In re Rebecca B., 227 A.D.2d 315 (N.Y. App. 1996), a child custody case, holding that the child's communications with her law guardian "as well as with the social worker hired by the Law Guardian" were protected by the attorney-client privilege or work product doctrine and that subpoenas served upon the law guardian and social worker were properly quashed.	NY
NC	G.S. §7B-301	§7B-301(B) - MISD.	Yes, "any person": §7B-301(a) any person		No, attorneys exempted: §7B-310	§7B-310 - all privileges abrogated, except attorney-client.	§7B-301(a) - cause to suspect		NC

(Continued)

State >	Mandatory Reporting Statute	Penalty for Failure to Report	"All Persons" are Reporters	"Social Workers" are Reporters	"Attorneys" are Reporters	Privileges: Recognized & Abrogated	Standard of Knowledge	Notes	State <
ND	N.D. Cent. Code 50-25.1-03	50-25.1-13 - MISD.		Yes: 50-25.1-03(1)	No: 50-25.1-03.1-1	50-25.1-10 - spousal and professional privileges abrogated, attorney-client privilege recognized.	50-25.1-03(1) - knowledge of or reasonable cause to suspect		ND
OH	ORC §2151.421	§2151.99 - MISD.		Yes: §2151.421(A)(1)(b)	Yes: §2151.421(A)(1)(b)	2151.421(A)(2) - attorney-client privilege recognized, but privilege is deemed waived for certain vulnerable persons by §2151.421(A)(3).	2151.421(A)(1)(a) - knows or has reasonable cause to suspect		OH
OK	10A O.S. §1-2-101	§1-2-101(C) - MISD. (if not prompt); possible FEL. (if prolonged knowledge of at least 6 months)	Yes, " every person": §1-2-101.B			§1-2-101.B.3 - all privileges abrogated.	1-2-101.B.1 - reason to believe		OK
OR	ORS 419B.010	419B.010(5) - Class A Violation	Yes, "any public or private official": 419B.010(1)	Yes, "regulated social worker": 419B.005(4)(i)	Yes: 419B.005(4)(m)	419B.010(1) - psychiatrist/psychologist-patient, clergy-pentitent, and attorney-client privilege recognized; ORS 40.225(2) - attorney-client privilege includes lawyers' representatives.	419B.010(1) - reasonable cause to believe		OR
PA	23 Pa.C.S. §6311	§6319 - MISD. unless the child abuse constitutes a felony of the first degree or higher, then failure to report is a felony		Yes, person licensed or certified to practice in any health-related field under PA Dept of State: § 6311(a)(1)	Yes, for attorneys affilaited with an agency, inst, or org responsible for children: §6311(a)(14)	§6311.1(b) - clergy-pentient and attorney-client privileges recognized; attorney professional responsibility rules recgonized.	§6311(a) - reasonable cause to suspect		PA

State >	Mandatory Reporting Statute	Penalty for Failure to Report	"All Persons" are Reporters	"Social Workers" are Reporters	"Attorneys" are Reporters	Privileges: Recognized & Abrogated	Standard of Knowledge	Notes	State <
RI	R.I. Gen. Laws §40-11-3	§40-11-6.1 - MISD. (fine &/or prison); CIVIL liability	Yes, "any person": §40-11-3(a)			§40-11-11 - spousal and professional privileges abrogated, attorney-client privilege recognized.	40-11-3(a) reasonable cause to know or suspect		RI
SC	S.C. Code Ann. §63-7-310	§63-7-410 - MISD. (up to 6 months imprisonment &/or $500 fine)		Yes, "social or public assistance worker": §63-7-310(A)		§63-7-420 - spousal and professional privileges abrogated, but clergy-penitent and attorney-client privilege recognized.	§63-7-310(B) - reason to believe		SC
SD	S.D. Codified Laws §26-8A-3	§26-8A-3 - Class 1 MISD.		Yes: §26-8A-3			§26-8A-3 - reasonable cause to suspect		SD
TN	Tenn. Code Ann. §37-1-403	§37-1-412 - MISD.	Yes, "any person": §37-1-403(a)(1)			§37-1-411. - spousal and psychiatrist/psychologist-patient privileges abrogated for some cases.	§37-1-403(a)(1) - "knowledge of" that which "reasonably appears to have been caused by brutality, abuse or neglect"		TN
TX	Tex. Fam. Code §261.101	§261.109 - MISD.	Yes, "a person": §261.101	Yes: §261.101(c)	Yes: §261.101(c)	§261.101(c) - attorney-client privilege recognized for evidence, but all privileges abrogated as to reporting.	§261.201(a) - cause to believe		TX
UT	Utah Code Ann. §62A-4a-403	§62A-4a-411 - MISD.	Yes, "any person": §62A-4a-403(1)(a)			§62A-4a-412(5) - physician-patient privilege abrogated, other privileges not mentioned.	§62A-4a-403(1)(a) - reason to believe		UT
VT	33 V.S.A. §4913	§4913(h) - up to $500 fine; if intent to conceal, up to $1000 fine &/or 6 months in prison		Yes: §4913(a)(5)	No: §4913(a)	§4913(j) - all privileges abrogated, except clergy-penitent privilege.	§4913(c) - reasonably suspects		V

(Continued)

State >	Mandatory Reporting Statute	Penalty for Failure to Report	"All Persons" are Reporters	"Social Workers" are Reporters	"Attorneys" are Reporters	Privileges: Recognized & Abrogated	Standard of Knowledge	Notes	State <
VA	Va. Code Ann. §63.2-1509	§ 63.2-1509(D) - 1st time, up to $500 fine; from thereon, up to $1000 fine; for sex offenses, MISD.		Yes: §63.2-1509(A)(3)	No: §63.2-1509(A)(1-18)	§ 63.2-1519 - spousal and physician-patient privileges abrogated	§63.2-1509(A) - reason to suspect		VA
WA	RCW §26.44.030	§26.44.080 - GROSS MISD.		Yes, "social service counselor": §26.44.030(1)(a)	No: §26.44.030(1)(a -b)	§26.44.030(1)(b) - all privileges recognized; §5.60.060 recognizes privilege as to (2)(a) counsel and (9) social worker.	§26.44.030(1)(a)) - reasonable cause to believe		WA
WV	WV Code §49-2-803	§49-2-812 - for abuse and neglect, MISD. (up to $5,000 fine &/or 90 days jail); for sexual assault or abuse, MISD. (up to $10,000 fine &/or 6 months jail)		Yes, "social services worker": §49-2-803(a)			§49-2-803(a) - reasonable cause to suspect		WV
WI	Wis. Stat. §48.981	§48.981(6) - up to $1,000 fine &/or 6 months jail		Yes: §48.981(2)(a)(10)			§48.981(2)(a) - reasonable cause to suspect		WI
WY	Wyo. Stat. §14-3-205		Yes, "any person": §14-3-205(a)			§14-3-210(a)(ii) - clergy-penitent and attorney-client privileges recognized.	§14-3-205(a) - knows or has reasonable cause to believe or suspect		WY

References

American Bar Association, Center for Professional Responsibility. (2013). *Model rules of professional conduct*. Retrieved from http://www.americanbar.org/groups/professional_responsiblity/publications/model_rules_of_professional_conduct.html

Andrews, A.B. (2012). American Bar Association supplementary guidelines for the mitigation function of defense teams in death penalty cases: Implications for social work. *Social Work*, *57*(2), 155–164.

Bergman, B.E., & N. Hollander. (2011). 3 Wharton's criminal evidence 15th ed. sec. 11:29.

Buchanan, S., & Nooe, R.M., (2017). Defining social work within holistic public defense: Challenges and implications for practice. *Social Work*, *62*(4), 333–339. doi: 10.1093/sw/swx032

BB v. People 785 P.2d 132, 137–138 (Colo 1990).

Campaign for the Fair Sentencing of Youth (CFSY). (2015). Retrieved from https://www.fairsentencingofyouth.org/media-resources/defense-guidelines/

Colorado Juvenile Defender Center & Colorado Alternate Defense Counsel Juvenile Defense Manual, 3rd Ed. (2018). Dianna Richett primary author. Stacie Colling and Amanda Butler prime Editors of the 3rd Edition.

Colorado Revised Statutes Section 19-2-517 (2012).

Colorado Rules of Professional Conduct Rule 1.6 (a) & (b). Confidentiality of Information. (2018). The Colorado Rules of professional conduct as adopted by the Colorado Supreme Court on May 7, 1992, effective January 1, 1993, as amended through rule change 2018(3), effective February 22, 2018.

Gideon v. Wainwright, 372 U.S. 335 (1963).

Griffin, P., Addie, S., Adams, B., & Firestine, K. (2011). Trying Juveniles as adults: An analysis of state transfer laws and reporting U.S. department of justice office of justice programs. *Office of Juvenile Justice and Delinquency Prevention*. Retrieved from https://www.ncjrs.gov/pdffiles1/ojjdp/232434.pdf

Hisle, B., Shdaimah, C.S., & Finegar, N. (2012). Neighborhood defenders program: An evaluation of Maryland's holistic representation program. *Journal of Forensic Social Work*, *2*, 122–140.

In Re Gault, 387 U.S. 1 (1967).

Kent v. United States, 383 U.S. 541 (1966).

Losavio v. Dist. Court, 533 P.2d 32, 35 (Colo. 1975).

Miller v. Alabama, 567 U.S. 460 (2012).

Montgomery v. Louisiana, 577 U.S. –, 136 S. Ct. 718 (2016).

National Association of Social Workers (NASW). (2018). http://www.socialworkers.org

National Association of Public Defense. (2018). Guiding principles. Retrieved from http://www.publicdefenders.us/?q=guiding-principles

National Association of Public Defense. (2014). *Formal ethics opinion addressing the confidentiality of client information when defense team representation includes social workers and other non-lawyer professionals whose licensure is affected by statutory or professional mandatory reporting obligations*. Retrieved from http://www.publicdefenders.us/files/NAPD_Formal_Ethics_Opinion_14-1.pdf. National Association of Public Defense: Ethics Opinion 14-1.

National Juvenile Defender Center (NJDC). (2012). National Juvenile Defense Standards. Retrieved from http://njdc.info/wp-content/uploads/2013/09/NationalJuvenileDefenseStandards2013.pdf

National Legal Aid and Defender Association (NLADA). (2016). Mandatory Reporting by State, *The Interdisciplinary Defense Team & Confidentiality: What Defenders Need to Know*

People v. Angel, 277 P.3d 231 (Colo. 2012).

People v. Johnson, 999 P. 2d 825 (Colo. 2000).

People v. Madera, 112 P.3d 688 (Colo. 2005).

Rule 1.6, Confidentiality of information. (2013). In American Bar Association, center for professional responsibility. (2013). *Model rules of professional conduct.* Retrieved from http://www.americanbar.org/groups/professional_responsiblity/publications/model_rules_of_professional_conduct/rule_1_6_confidentiality_of_information.html

Rule 5.3, Responsibilities Regarding non-lawyer Assistance. (2013). In American Bar Association, center for professional responsibility. (2013). *Model rules of professional conduct.* Retrieved from https://www.americanbar.org/groups/professional_responsibility/publications/model_rules_of_professional_conduct/rule_5_3_responsibilities_regarding_nonlawyer_assistant.html

Senna, J.J. (1975). Social workers in public defender programs. *Social Work*, *20*, 271–277.

Wald, M. (1972). *The use of social workers in a public defender office: An evaluation of the offender rehabilitation project of the public defender office for Santa Clara County, California.* San Jose, CA: Office of the Public Defender.

3

ROLES OF THE FORENSIC SOCIAL WORKER

Molly Hennessey and Maren Willins

Abstract

This chapter will provide an overview of the roles relevant to a criminal defense-based forensic social worker. There are many different practice models of a forensic social worker. This chapter will focus on the "employee model" and the roles needed at the micro, mezzo and macro levels. These roles will be explored within case study examples.

Learning Objectives

- Understand the roles of a criminal defense-based forensic social worker within an employee practice model
- Identify and define several micro-, mezzo-, and macro-level forensic social work roles
- Relate these roles to a case study example

The profession of social work covers a vast number of fields and areas of specialty, going far beyond the assumption that social workers only work in the child protection system. Social workers are employed in a variety of areas, including (but not limited to) hospitals, community mental health, schools, correctional systems, treatment centers, political advocacy agencies, the court system, nonprofits, etc. There is a long history of social workers working within the legal system, dating back 1899 when the first juvenile courts were established in Chicago (Roberts & Bronwell, 1999).

Social work scholars have historically defined forensic social work as the intersection of social work and the legal system. This definition can be applied to any social workers working within the criminal, juvenile, and civil court systems. The National Organization for Forensic Social Work (NOFSW) defines the area as "the application of social work to questions and issues relating to law and legal systems."

Common areas of the legal system social workers operate in can include public defense (both criminal and civil), the child welfare system, involuntary mental health commitments, court-ordered treatment, divorce proceedings, victim and child advocacy, the juvenile justice systems, and adult corrections (NOFSW, n.d.).

This chapter will focus on the many roles of the forensic social workers working specifically on criminal defense teams. Social workers who are employed on legal defense teams will be referred to as *forensic social workers*. The utilization of social workers on legal defense teams has evolved over the years, based on the identified needs of the client populations. *Holistic, comprehensive*, and *collaborative* are just a few words frequently used to describe the movement toward integrating social workers as multidisciplinary members of legal defense teams. There can be various professionals with different expertise on legal teams and it is becoming more and more common to have social workers working alongside attorneys on cases.

The Center for Holistic Defense (2015) defines holistic defense as:

> An innovative, client-centered, and interdisciplinary model of public defense that addresses both the circumstances driving people into the justice systems as well as the devastating consequences of that court involvement. Based on individual needs, this model connects clients with criminal defense, family defense, and related civil legal representation, as well as social work support and advocacy beyond the courtroom.

As part of a holistic defense team, the forensic social worker "wears many hats" and will take on different roles and duties depending on the case and the needs of the client. The forensic social worker will operate as a multidisciplinary team member. Roles are based on the needs identified by the legal team, the client, and the forensic social worker. Roles should be considered a dynamic aspect of the legal team, as they may change over the course of the case.

The lead attorney on the case will help define the role(s) the forensic social worker will take for the case. Role definition is critical in this work. It is essential that the forensic social worker has input and advocacy around the roles she or he will take on the team. Oftentimes, defense teams will have multiple other professionals assisting on the team and filling different roles. For example, paralegals, investigators, legal assistants, and experts may all be working together on a defense team. It is necessary to identify and clarify the different roles on the teams, so efforts are not duplicated. Furthermore, social workers have a special skill set that should be utilized and capitalized upon, making them an important asset on defense-based legal teams. These specific skills are discussed later in Chapter 4, "Skills." In addition, these roles and duties should be revisited over the course of the case as the needs of the client and/or the case may change over time.

Practice Models Within Defense-Based Social Work

It is important to identify the practice model your agency utilizes, as it will inform your potential roles with the legal defense team. The National Association of Social Workers (NASW) recognizes six different ways forensic social workers are utilized on legal teams and in the legal system. Each model carries duties and obligations, or a combination.

- The consult model: a forensic social worker who works with an attorney as an expert consultant. No direct client services are provided with this model.
- The direct service provider: in this model the forensic social worker works as an internal referral source within a legal agency.
- The employee model: in the employee model, the forensic social worker is an employee of the lawyer or law firm representing the client.
- The consent model: this model asks that clients agree to the social worker disclosing child protection concerns.
- The confidentiality wall model: this model utilizes an early screening by the lawyer(s) to identify any child abuse issues prior to involving a social worker.
- The notice model: in this model agencies will notify clients of the social workers ethical obligations to report child protection issues before engaging with a forensic social worker.

(NASW, 2006)

This book will focus on the employee model, referenced earlier. The NASW identifies this as the forensic social worker working as an agent or employee of the attorney appointed to the case. The attorney may identify the need for a forensic social worker at the beginning of or further along in the case. In the employee model, the attorney acts as the leader of the defense team while guiding and collaborating with the forensic social worker, investigator, paralegal or legal assistant, and the client. Forensic social workers can fulfill a variety of functions and are an important asset to the defense team. The attorney appointed to the case may identify the need for a forensic social worker based on a variety of reasons, which can include serious charges, mental health concerns, the need for resource identification and connection, and many more. Based on the agency setting, a forensic social worker may be requested from within the agency or as an independent contractor.

When working within the "employee model," the forensic social worker must follow attorney-client privilege and confidentiality rules. Ethical considerations will be discussed further in Chapter 2, "Guiding Principles of Practice." As an employee or agent of the attorney, the social worker must take direction from the attorney(s) on the case and must *always* represent the goals of the team through their defense work on behalf of the client and the team.

An agency may adopt one practice model or may take different aspects of each to form models that meet the needs of their client population. It is extremely important for the agency utilizing the forensic social worker and the forensic social worker to identify and agree upon the model for and expectations of the social worker. This way, the social worker and attorneys can both understand the role of the forensic social worker.

Roles of the Forensic Social Worker on Holistic Defense Teams

Social scientists and social work scholars have listed and defined the many roles of a forensic social worker (Bronx Defenders, 2015; Buchanan & Nooe, 2017; NOFSW, n.d.; Steinberg, 2013). These roles extend across micro, mezzo, and macro levels of social work. While some of the following roles are well defined by other experts in the forensic social work field, this chapter seeks to elaborate on these roles and propose additional roles.

- Advocate for the client with family, the legal team, various services and systems they operate within, and on macro levels.
- Service connecter and navigator: Clients in the legal system frequently have unmet needs or may not be connected to appropriate and relevant services. When working with clients in the community, help obtain documents (e.g., identification) and make referrals to treatment, inpatient services, mental health services, case management, etc. depending on services available in the community.
- Assessment/evaluator: Identifying presenting issues, mitigating factors, and performing ongoing evaluation. Assess for unmet needs, including substance abuse, trauma, mental health, and medical issues. Also, assess for cognitive, developmental, and intellectual disabilities. Finally, evaluate for appropriate community services as well as the necessary level of services.
- Mitigation investigator: Interviewing relevant witnesses and collateral contacts, identifying, collecting, and analyzing records. This information is used to humanize the client and to help inform the social worker for a release or reentry plan, in addition to in the identification of mitigating factors and help with theorizing defense strategy. Many times, clients are only viewed within the context of the alleged crime. Mitigation is a

chance to bring a client's story to life and present the facts with compassion and understanding, as well as allowing the client to be the "expert" of their life. Conduct comprehensive and complete biopsychosocial interviews and assessments. Create and present persuasive reports and visuals to present to district attorneys, judges, or juries. An example of a visual would be a genogram showing family dynamics, a time line of important life events, or a family photo album.
- Therapeutic and emotional support: Provide crisis intervention, support, and psychoeducation to clients.
- Release planner: Propose strategies and community services to support the client to either reenter the community or avoid an incarceration sentence.
- Social scientist and researcher: Research and summarize relevant research in the social science fields for mitigation purposes. Use social science research to mitigate difficult facts and behaviors and recommend specific treatment or alternative sentences.
- Consultant on the legal team: Consult regarding client needs, advise how the team can best communicate with and support client. Identify the need for expert(s) to consult, prepare an assessment/evaluation, and/or provide expert testimony.
- Liaison between legal team and client's family and loved ones.
- Expert witness: Provide testimony based on records reviewed, interviews conducted with witnesses, relevant firsthand observations, and interactions with client.

While many of the roles outlined here are on the micro (individual) level of social work, there is important work to be done on the mezzo and macro levels. Forensic social workers advocate every day for their clients within the courtroom, at facilities, with court professionals, and with service providers, and they can also bring their advocacy to lawmakers, legislative hearings, and the general community. Forensic social workers have invaluable insight in the issues and discriminatory policies and laws their clients face every day. Some examples of mezzo- and macro-level roles can include the following.

Mezzo Roles

- Provide trainings within the social worker's own agency and within the professional community. A forensic social worker can give professional or informational trainings to various audiences who interact with forensic populations. Examples could include community resource agencies, schools, local police departments, mental health providers, residential facilities, and those within the social worker own organization.
- Advocate within your own agency to address any barriers faced by clients and/or their families.

- Work within your own agency to improve the environment and culture for both clients and employees.

Macro Roles

- Involvement in policy advocacy in legislation process. For example, attend meetings and legislative hearings, testify, help to give a voice to clients, and advocate for systemic changes.
- Program development: Forensic social workers can help consult to help other programs grow as well as review their effectiveness and client reach.
- Provide training and informational sessions to the greater community: Provide trainings to national audiences on forensic social work on topics related to forensic populations including barriers faced by this population, best practices, emerging research, etc.
- Raise awareness through advocacy for issues and the need for reform in criminal justice system on topics such as racial disparities, high imprisonment rates in United States, length of sentence, overcrowding, use of solitary confinement, treatment of mental illness, and reentry.
- Behavioral science research: Forensic social workers could contribute to the academic community through research, writing, and conducting studies to inform practice, agency evaluation, and best practices (NOFSW, n.d.).

Case Studies

Read the case studies and consider which role(s) the forensic social worker may take in each case. Examples of appropriate roles are discussed later. As previously discussed, the roles of the forensic social worker are dynamic and may change over the course of the case.

Case Study #1 (Ben)

Ben is a 22-year-old male with symptoms of severe anxiety, including difficulty concentrating, racing thoughts, heart palpitations, sleep problems, nightmares, and weight loss. These symptoms started when he entered jail about 2 months ago. Ben has a history of experiencing similar symptoms of anxiety in his teenage years but never received a formal mental health diagnosis. You suspect that Ben is suffering from generalized anxiety disorder related to past and current trauma. Ben is not taking any medications and has no other medical concerns.

Ben's charges are kidnapping, theft of a motor vehicle, and second-degree manslaughter. When he was 16 years old, Ben was in juvenile court for two Driving While Ability Impaired (DWAI) tickets, truancy, and misdemeanor trespassing. His current charges are Ben's first felonies. The incident that Ben was arrested for revolves around an alleged gang house party. During this party, a vehicle was stolen, and a male victim sustained serious bodily injury and died in the hospital 2 days after he was admitted.

You know that Ben originally got involved in a gang (the Bloods) because of his father, who is an Original Gangster (OG). Ben was jumped in at age 14. He grew up in poverty and around pervasive community violence. You do not yet know the extent of violence and trauma that Ben was exposed to, but you suspect that there is a significant amount. While there is nothing in the medical records about traumatic brain injury (TBI), you suspect that Ben has had at least two concussions. Ben's parents were married shortly after his birth and divorced when Ben was 10 years old. He has two younger siblings, aged 18 and 14. Their father is married to Ben's mom.

Ben is not married and has no children. Ben completed his General Educational Development Certificate (GED) at age 20 and has some work experience in the fast food industry. He has an interest in the culinary arts and aspires to move further in this field. Ben's father was also arrested on charges related to this incident. Ben's mother visits Ben in jail weekly.

Ben's attorneys would like you to provide emotional support to Ben while he is incarcerated, assess his mental health needs, and work with him and the jail to provide mental health treatment. Additionally, the attorneys would like you to explore his family, community, academic, medical, psychological, and employment history, and conceptualize it into a court report.

- **Therapeutic support and building rapport:** The attorney is requesting that the forensic social worker supports the client while he is incarcerated.
- **Service connection:** It may be beneficial for the client to be connected with the mental health or psychiatry department in the jail if his mental health and sleeping disorder persist. In addition, if there is a possibility that the client could be released on bond or receive a community sentence, it would be necessary to assist the client with setting up supportive services to help him live successfully in the community. This could include making a referral to a community mental health agency, a mentorship program, and/or a group support program. These services would help support him with ongoing

mental health and psychiatry services. If/when Ben is released back into the community, it may be appropriate to help him explore options for a culinary arts program, as that was an expressed interest and would help address his employment and educational needs.

- **Mitigation investigation**: There are multiple indications within the case study that a thorough mitigation investigation is warranted besides the attorney making that initial request. Not only is Ben a young person facing very serious charges and a potentially lengthy sentence; there are additional mentions of mitigating factors, such as mental health symptoms, prior criminal history, gang involvement, vocational and educational factors, parental criminality, and potential brain injuries, to name a few. Additionally, the mitigation investigation should include a complete record search and collection. This information can help tell Ben's story and humanize him within the context of his case, helping the prosecutor and/or judge understand the client's life. This historical information could also help inform you of an appropriate reentry plan and what may help meet Ben's needs that were not addressed previously.
- **Consultation and advocacy with legal team**: If an initial evaluation/assessment of Ben reveals mental health symptoms, requesting an expert or mental health evaluation may be appropriate. Considering consulting with an expert in TBIs may be another helpful resource on this case.

Case Study #2 (Deb)

Deb is a 30-year-old, African American female with a developmental disability and an IQ of 65. She is originally from an impoverished neighborhood in Detroit, Michigan. She and her mother moved to Colorado when Deb was 14 years old to get distance from some of their other family members. Deb was briefly married at age 18 years and divorced 2 years later. She has no children but has a dog she cares for by feeding him, walking him, and keeping him healthy. Deb has not completed high school and quit going to school at age 16. She has a history of theft; most of her charges were relatively minor, without any jail time. Currently, she violated her probation because she is having difficulty keeping track of her court and probation appointments. After her most recent arrest, Deb lost her job at the grocery store where she has worked for the past 5 years.

Deb is working with the same attorney who helped her during her previous legal issues 2 years ago. Her attorney secured a Personal Recognizance bond for Deb who is currently living at her mother's house. Deb has been living with her aging mom, who is an alcoholic, for all of her life. Deb's attorney would like you to help Deb find more appropriate housing and "whatever else she needs."

Deb has various school and medical records that her attorney would like you to review. It will not only be important to obtain records for Deb, but Individualized Education Plan (IEP) records will also provide greater details about her specific learning and developmental difficulties. As you review these records you learn that several times during her childhood the Department of Human Services (DHS) investigated alleged abuse against Deb by her mother's boyfriend at the time. You know from the DHS records that one of her mom's boyfriends sexually abused Deb for about 8 months when she was 11 years old. Deb's school records reveal that she was in special education since Kindergarten and connected with the Arc, an agency devoted to assisting people with intellectual and developmental disabilities, beginning at age 8.

When you first meet with Deb at her mother's house, you smell alcohol on her mother. She excused herself and stayed in her room for the remainder of your visit. After explaining who you are and your role as a forensic social worker, Deb asks, "Do you want to hear about when my mom's boyfriend had sex with me?"

- **Assessment and evaluation:** The forensic social worker should meet with the client to assess their needs and also potential mitigating factors and/or witnesses to interview. It appears Deb has unmet needs. Since Deb has violated her probation, the forensic social worker should assess for gaps in previous services and additional relevant and appropriate services.
- **Mitigation investigation and record collection/review:** Gathering additional records may reveal new sources to request records from. Sometimes, our clients are not the best historians and reviewing their records can lead us to extra helpful information.
- **Advocacy and consultation with the attorney:** Although the previous attorney has worked with Deb before, it may be helpful to consult the attorney on developmentally appropriate communication with Deb. This will help the attorney communication with the client and Deb will hopefully feel heard and understood by her attorney. This can also help the social worker assess for any potential competency issues.

- **Service connection:** It is important for the forensic social worker to assess Deb for relevant and appropriate services within the community. The forensic social worker should work with Deb to advocate and help Deb meet her personal goals. Deb may also be eligible for additional services she is not already connected with (e.g., state benefits or Social Security funds) that may assist her in living independently if Deb chooses not to continue living with her mother. Deb also confided with her forensic social worker about past abuse, so a referral to a mental health agency may be appropriate if Deb wishes to seek counseling for her trauma.

Practical Tips

- Keep in regular contact with the attorney(s) on your case. Communication is key!
- If you are unsure of the role(s) on the case, clarify with your team immediately.
- Send your teams regular or semi-regular updates, so they are aware of what you are working on, any issues you have encountered, and progress working toward long-term tasks.
- Request periodical in-person team meetings.
- Develop a system for documenting your work on the case.
- Maintain an organized case file and document all communication related to the case, whether it is email, texts, phone calls, attempted calls, visits, etc.

Conclusion

There are many various roles associated with a criminal defense-based forensic social worker. Understanding the agency and community in which the forensic social worker is employed will help to further clarify the roles. These roles may vary based on the micro, mezzo and macro levels of forensic social work. Based on the employee model of practice, the forensic social worker is an agent of the attorney and will function under the same attorney-client privilege and confidentiality rules.

References

Bronx Defenders. (2015). *The Center for Holistic Defense*. Retrieved from http://www.bronxdefenders.org/holistic-defense/center-for-holistic-defense/

Buchanan, S., & Nooe, R.M. (2017). Defining social work within holistic public defense: Challenges and implications for practice. *Social Work, 62*(4). *33–339.* doi: 10.1093/sw/swx032

National Association of Social Workers (NASW). (2006). Legal and ethical issues in social work Lawyer collaborations. https://www.socialworkers.org/ldf/legal_issue/200801.aspback=yes

National Organization of Forensic Social Work (NOFSW) (2018). Nofsw.org.

Roberts, A.R., & Bronwell, P. (1999). A century of forensic social work: Bridging the past to the present. *Social Work, 44*(4), 359–369.

Steinberg, R. (2013). Heeding Gideon's call in the twenty-first century: Holistic defense and the new public defense paradigm. *Washington and Lee Law Review, 70*(2), 1–33.

4

SKILLS

Maren Willins and Hillary Vervalin

Abstract

This chapter will provide an overview of the skills needed by a criminal defense-based forensic social worker. While some forensic social worker skills overlap with traditional social work skills, many are unique to this role. Clinical, collaborative, and practical forensic social work skills will be introduced and defined. These skills will also be incorporated into case study examples.

Learning Objectives

- Understand which skills are unique to the criminal defense-based forensic social worker
- Identify and define several clinical, collaborative, and practical skills
- Relate these skills to a case study example

Practitioners of criminal defense-based forensic social work navigate complex multifaceted systems at all practice levels, including working with individuals experiencing incarceration, advocating for clients in the courtroom, and promoting systemic efforts in criminal justice reform. Forensic social workers will find themselves tasked with managing and evaluating clients, conducting intensive social science research, identifying community resources, testifying in court, and/or testifying to the state legislature. There are several important and varied skills that a criminal defense-based forensic social worker must possess in order to effectively complete his or her job. This chapter will cover the knowledge and skills utilized by forensic social workers in various criminal defense-based cases and defense teams.

While forensic social work practice is exciting, can help individual clients, and creates systemic change in the criminal justice system, it also presents unique practice challenges. Forensic social workers must have the skills to bridge the gap between sociological models and criminological practice. A fundamental skill of defense-based forensic social workers is the ability to think creatively and collaboratively while remaining client-centered. Furthermore, forensic social workers must have a distinctive combination of strong clinical abilities, assessment skills, the aptitude to present the complexity of a client's story, knowledge of community resources, and the ability to collaborate with a team.

Clinical

Building Rapport (Client and Family Level)

A criminal defense-based forensic social worker must have well-developed clinical skills to build rapport with diverse clients in both the community and detention facilities, as well as with their clients' families and support systems. It is imperative for the forensic social worker to build a rapport with the client which leads to the client trusting in the social worker over time. Effective rapport begins by "communicating with empathy and authenticity" (Hepworth, Rooney, & Larson, 2002, p. 87). The client must have enough trust in their social worker to feel comfortable providing personal, and often sensitive, information. "The social worker uses communication skills as building blocks to assist in the development of a productive working relationship" (Hepworth, et al., 2002, p. 92). A criminal defense-based social worker is building a relationship with the client that will help the social worker accurately assess past or present sources of trauma, current functioning, past and/or present mental illness, past or current substance use, and developmental delays, among other things, all of which may provide mitigation and aid in the client's defense. The forensic social worker is also identifying support systems, clarifying what may be needed upon reentry and more. These tasks cannot be accomplished without establishing a trusting relationship.

In many instances, especially with juvenile clients, building rapport with a client's family may be as important as doing so with the client, although the client is always the social worker's priority. A client's family may be his or her biggest support and their family history and dynamics may be complex. Family and support systems hold valuable information regarding the client. Appropriate relationships with family members may be key to supporting the client, learning the client's history, building mitigation, and designing future reentry plans.

Case Study #3 (Rodrigo)

Rodrigo is a 16-year-old male who experienced significant abuse and neglect in the foster care system as a child. He was separated from his brother at the age of 3, and they grew up moving frequently to different foster homes. From the Department of Human Services records, you learn that many different therapists and caseworkers have been assigned to Rodrigo's case. There are literally several hundred pages of records that the attorneys ask you to review, cross-reference, and summarize for an expert in developmental psychology.

Rodrigo is facing first-degree murder charges in adult court. A reverse-transfer hearing is scheduled in 8 months. The lead attorney wants you to review the lengthy discovery (police reports, witness interviews, etc.) about the alleged incident. In addition to summarizing the records for the expert, the defense team would like you to provide emotional support to Rodrigo while he remains in a juvenile detention facility.

In speaking with Rodrigo, he describes issues with bullying which he says led him to carry a gun "to protect myself." Rodrigo continues to express grief over the "loss" of his brother at a young age and wants you to find him. You eventually learn that one of Rodrigo's first foster families was neglectful and abusive. Rodrigo has a close connection with his most recent foster mother who tries her best to visit him monthly. His biological family is from a rural area of Mexico, and several family members who live near where Rodrigo is being detained are Spanish-speaking only.

Rodrigo's defense team wants the forensic social worker to support Rodrigo during this process of court proceedings in adult court as a juvenile and to also interview all of his biological family members and his foster family. Furthermore, the attorneys want the forensic social worker to build a mitigation packet in time for the reverse-transfer hearing to assist in keeping Rodrigo's cases in juvenile court. If/when this goal is met, the defense team will want the social worker to expand upon the mitigation packet to address alternative placement and treatment options to the court.

Case Study Discussion

As a forensic social worker on this case, connecting with Rodrigo and his family is both crucial and complicated. Rodrigo is a client who likely has been disappointed by the professionals in his past. He was separated from his brother at a young age and indicates he blames the "social worker who took my brother away from me." It is also important to consider that Rodrigo is a 16-year-old male who isn't talkative with his peers or adults. Rodrigo is not the type of client who is going to open up immediately or quickly. From a cultural perspective, it is ideal to have a bilingual forensic social worker on the defense team if possible as he or she could more effectively communicate with Rodrigo's family.

Strategies for building rapport with Rodrigo and his family include taking things slowly and adequately explaining the role of a criminal defense-based social worker and how that differs from other social workers that Rodrigo and his family may have interacted with in the past. Collateral information collected from school and social service records will be important in understanding the part of Rodrigo's history that he may not remember and/or that his family is uncomfortable with sharing. In collecting collateral information, the social worker may uncover a foster parent or therapist whom Rodrigo truly trusted. The social worker can ask Rodrigo about this person including what he or she did that Rodrigo valued, which can provide the social worker with ways to better connect with him. This person may be a good source of information regarding Rodrigo's life history and should be interviewed if possible. This person might also be able to provide Rodrigo with support following his arrest.

Clinical Interviewing

Next, a criminal defense-based social worker should possess effective clinical interviewing skills. Clinical interviewing utilizes open-ended questions, motivational interviewing, nonjudgmental responses, and engaged body language. Forensic social workers should also be competent in identifying the somatic, emotional, and psychological signs of trauma in a client. According to Kadushin and Kadushin (2012), "social workers spend more time interviewing than in any other single activity. It is the most important and most frequently used social work skill" (p. 14). Motivational interviewing is a type of interviewing that helps individuals overcome ambivalence to effect change in their lives (Miller & Rollnick, 2002). This skill can be especially important when working with the criminal justice population and building the motivation for change in your client, so they may better take care of themselves, reduce recidivism, and engage in pro-social activities, all while remaining a productive member of their community (Miller & Rollnick, 2002).

Child and adolescent psychologist Dr. Margaret Beyer has evaluated hundreds of juveniles who were charged in juvenile court or adult court (direct file, transfer, and reverse-transfer cases), or were sentenced to life without the possibility of parole as juveniles but are now adults (called juvenile life without parole (JLWOP) cases). Dr. Beyer has implemented a type of assessment called the developmental assessment to evaluate juvenile and JLWOP clients (JLWOP clients are evaluated retrospectively because a developmental assessment was not done at the time of the original case). It is similar to the kind of comprehensive biopsychosocial assessments that a forensic social worker completes for most cases. A biopsychosocial assessment is an evaluation tool that takes into account biological, psychological, and social factors relevant to a person's life history. Similarly, the developmental assessment looks at factors that have impacted an individual during the childhood and adolescent developmental processes. Dr. Beyer's insights and skills utilized to formulate a developmental assessment will be included and cited accordingly throughout this chapter.

Social History Formation

As explained earlier, over time, the criminal defense-based social worker builds rapport and a trusting relationship with the client, their family, and/or their network of support. The relationship with the client, and ideally the family, makes the social worker the most appropriate person to obtain the client's life history. Moreover, the social worker is the professional on the defense team most qualified to understand the client's life history in the context of how certain events and circumstances may have negatively impacted the individual during important, developmental stages. Ideally, the social worker becomes involved in the case shortly after the client is arrested and remains actively involved on the defense team for the duration of the case. The forensic social worker's ongoing involvement on the legal team permits him or her to obtain the client's life-history information slowly and methodically over many weeks or months. This is also beneficial for the client, who may need a substantial amount of time to develop a trusting, professional relationship with the social worker before sharing their most personal, and often traumatic, experiences. It is also important to remember that the client may not have shared these personal and traumatic experiences with anyone else before or in many years. This generally increases the client's reluctance to speak freely and openly, at least initially.

For example, when the forensic social worker first asks Rodrigo about his upbringing, he explains that one of his first foster mothers was positive and supportive throughout his childhood. Once Rodrigo trusts his social worker and understands that the exchange of information is confidential, he discloses that this foster mother used drugs during his childhood. She was often not home when Rodrigo was young which allowed his foster father to frequently physically abuse him. If the forensic social worker had not taken the time to build rapport and a trusting relationship with Rodrigo, this traumatic and neglectful experience in his first foster home may not have been discovered.

According to Dr. Beyer, in a series of private interviews that make up the bulk of the developmental assessment, preferably occurring for several hours at a time and at various times on different days, the way the young person thinks, memories of the past, reflections about relationships and family life, school experiences, and their stated values will reveal important information. The interviewer has a list of topics to be covered by the end of the interviews but following the young person's lead is usually most productive. Sometimes, discussing past records with the young person can provide insight. Listening to the young person read a writing sample aloud and observing some math calculations are also helpful. The individual doing the developmental assessment must be sensitive to the unique developmental stories of girls, youth of color, and lesbian, gay, bisexual, transgender, questioning, queer (LGBTQ) youth, and interview in a respectful and thoughtful manner. This will be discussed more in depth in Chapter 5, "Cultural Humility and Special Populations." As the interviews progress, and based on record review, a detailed time line of the young person's life—including dates of traumatic losses and other experiences, such as changing caregivers and moving schools—can become a valuable tool for understanding the youth's development and the complexity behind his or her behavior. See Chapter 6, "Work Product," to learn how to create a time line. Depending on their training, the individual preparing the developmental assessment may use inventories, checklists, and other evaluative tools (bearing in mind culture, class, and gender bias) and may incorporate the findings from previous evaluations in telling the young person's story.

Interviewing the Family and Others Who Know the Young Person

After the criminal defense-based social worker obtains life-history information from the client, he or she then corroborates and builds upon that information by speaking with anyone in the client's life who has relevant information including family members, foster parents, treatment providers and in some cases, teachers, neighbors, and childhood friends.

Dr. Beyer explains that parents, grandparents, and other significant family members are interviewed, sometimes together and sometimes separately depending on what will be most informative. Preferably, family interviews occur after one or more interviews with the youth and before the completion of those youth interviews, so the individual doing the developmental assessment can clarify different perspectives. Interviewing family members in the home where the youth was living at the time of arrest can be revealing. Family insights about the young person's exposure to trauma and response, past treatment, school experiences, and relationships are informative even though they may differ from the written record. A genogram of the young person's immediate and extended family can be a valuable tool for understanding the youth's development. Additionally, coaches, pastors, teachers, probation staff, foster care workers, therapists, detention staff, and others may have insights about the young person that are important in doing a developmental assessment.

Records Review

While the forensic social worker interviews family members and other important figures in the client's life, he or she will also review all the available records about the client and his or her family. It is important to note that on some cases, it may be the social worker's role to request records. However, on many criminal defense teams, there is an investigator who is responsible for requesting records. It is still most appropriate for the social worker to review the records that pertain to the client's life history. Moreover, many social workers have experience in agency settings and can best decode and analyze record data. Important records to obtain include but are not limited to birth records, Department of Human Services records, foster care records, group home records, treatment center records, juvenile detention center records, and school records, especially special education records as they often yield more-detailed information about the client's IQ, cognitive and emotional functioning, school- and community-based interventions, family dynamics, etc. It is crucial that the social worker review any and all available records, as they contain information about life events while they were taking place or shortly thereafter. An account of events shortly after they took place can be a truer reflection of what happened in the client's life before variables such as memory, bias, perception, and the effects of trauma become factors for the client and the client's family members in the retelling of the story.

Additionally, records may provide details about prior victimization that family members or caretakers were unaware of or that the client either cannot remember or has blocked out as a coping mechanism. According to Ford, Chapman, Hawke, and Albert (2007), the juvenile and adult criminal justice systems contain a higher percentage of individuals who were victimized as children. "For those involved with the juvenile justice system, the prevalence of youth exposed to trauma is believed to be higher than that of community samples..." (p. 1).

Identifying and Analyzing Risk and Protective Factors

As the forensic social worker obtains the client's life history and reviews past records, he or she observes and takes note of retrospective, present, and future risk and protective factors. The terms "risk and protective factors" originated in the medical field. A risk factor was defined by the American Medical Association (AMA) as a variable that increases an individual's chance of developing a disease or condition. Conversely, a protective factor is a variable that decreases or minimizes an individual's likelihood of developing a disease and/or mitigates the risk factors present. The same medical definition for risk and protective factors can be applied to delinquency and criminal involvement (Office of the Surgeon General, 2001). When looking at past criminal involvement, a client's current charges, and/or determining the likelihood of recidivism, a risk factor is a variable in a person's life that has increased the probability of criminal involvement. Conversely, a protective factor is a variable that mitigates or reduces the risk of criminal involvement. Protective factors can directly mitigate present risk factors (i.e., a juvenile client who is struggling in school receives a tutor or a gang-involved adolescent works with a gang-outreach volunteer to leave the gang-life behind). On the other hand, a protective factor can add positive value to an individual's life without directly reducing a specific risk (i.e., a client has a multitude of risk factors, including familial conflict, parental drug use, and antisocial peers), but the juvenile works with a mentor and finds a new pro-social hobby that he or she enjoys. While these protective factors cannot directly help with the familial conflict or parental substance use, they still provide the individual with positive outlets and reduce the likelihood of subsequent, delinquent behavior (Youth.gov, n.d.).

A way to understand how risk factors accumulate and put a person at higher risk for negative life outcomes is the Adverse Childhood Experience (or ACE) Study. The ACE Study was originally created out of a partnership between the Center for Disease Control and Prevention and Kaiser Permanente's Health Appraisal Clinic in San Diego seeking to better understand the link between adverse childhood experiences (risk factors) and physical health and well-being in later life (Felitti et al., 2014). As the researchers continued to evaluate individuals, it became evident that adverse childhood experiences correlated with negative life outcomes far beyond physical health. The ACE Study found that a person who had one adverse childhood experience generally had many and that the quality of life for a person with four or more adverse childhood experiences (risk factors) decreased greatly. Those with four or more adverse childhood experiences were "twice as likely to smoke, 12 times more likely to attempt suicide, seven times more likely to be alcoholic, and 10 times more likely to inject street drugs." Additionally, those with a higher ACE score were at a "240 percent greater risk of hepatitis and sexually-transmitted disease" (ACE Study, 2014). Baglivio et al. found juveniles and young adults in the criminal justice system "had markedly higher prevalence rates" of adverse childhood experiences than community members in the initial ACE Study (2014, p. 4). This research indicates a correlation between maltreatment and instability in childhood and future involvement in criminal activity. The ACE Study exemplifies an important point when evaluating risk and protective factors for individuals; it is not always one particular risk factor that determines the likelihood someone will develop internalized or externalized negative behaviors in later years; it is an accumulation of risks that leaves an individual vulnerable (Coie et al., 1993; Herrenkohl et al., 2000).

As cited earlier, research asserts that it is generally a culmination or the compounding effects of risk factors and the absence of protective factors that create the greatest risk for individuals. For example, a juvenile who has one or two risk factors for criminal involvement, including antisocial peers and difficulty in school, yet numerous protective factors, including a supportive family, involvement in pro-social extracurricular activities like music or art, and a mentor, is less likely to get involved in delinquent behavior than a juvenile with only one or two protective factors and numerous risk factors, such as divorced parents, antisocial peers, difficulties in school, and living in an impoverished and unsafe neighborhood. It should be noted that certain risk factors are pervasive enough to outweigh most protective factors without appropriate treatment and/or intervention; examples are mental health issues, substance use, and gang involvement.

Dr. Beyer's Developmental Assessment

As stated, another way to evaluate a client's life experiences and how they have impacted the child's development is Dr. Beyer's development assessment. The following are a list of questions to ask and topics to review with the client during your interview.

1. What effects continue from trauma exposure in this youth's life?
    - Chronology of physical abuse, sexual abuse, exposure to violence, removal from home and other disrupted caregiving, loss of important individuals, bullying, discrimination, psychological maltreatment, and other life events
    - Difficulties with self-regulation (easily overstimulated, limited self-calming skills, getting quickly frustrated)
    - Fearfulness (being on constant alert)
    - Nightmares and/or intrusive bad memories
    - Numbing feelings and memories with substances
    - Trouble concentrating
    - Being controlling, especially when anxious
    - Unusual irritability
    - Depression/suicidal thinking
    - Self-protectiveness when feeling threatened (reactive alarm response)
    - Mistrusting others
    - Difficulty self-calming
    - Oversensitivity; unusual perception of others as hostile, mean, and/or unfair
    - When feelings are hurt, flooded with anger from the past out of proportion to the present provocation
    - Feeling picked-on or ostracized

- Self-dislike, self-blaming and attention-seeking
- Belligerent outspokenness
- Dissociation (unable to remember emotionally charged situations)

2. Does this young person have learning problems?
   (a) Problems processing information
   - Has trouble digesting what is said and/or written (including difficulty comprehending and following instructions and/or listening)
   - Has expressive or receptive language difficulties, including telling coherent narratives

   (b) Executive function deficits
   - Organizing, prioritizing, or sequencing

   (c) Characteristics of Autism Spectrum Disorder or fetal substance exposure?
   - Getting easily overstimulated
   - Oblivious to simple rules that other children routinely obey
   - Does not learn from experience, repeating the same mistakes
   - Seems younger than his/her chronological age

   (d) Does a diagnosis of ADD/ADHD adequately account for this young person's behavior?
   - Documentation of
     - attention/concentration difficulties/distractibility for child's age
     - high activity level for child's age and/or excessive daydreaming for child's age
   - What are the details of his/her poor social skills/problems with peers?
   - Has he/she had a diagnosis of ADD and ADHD? If medication did not produce improvement, was an alternative diagnosis given to account for attention difficulties and getting quickly frustrated (for example, the effects of trauma or the symptoms of mild autism that are similar)?

   (e) What accounts for discrepancies between reading/math skills and IQ subtest scores?

3. How specifically does this young person's behavior reflect his/her immature thinking?
   - Difficulty anticipating consequences/planning
   - Childish decision-making when scared and/or stressed (including seeing only one option)
   - Minimizing danger/not recognizing work possible outcomes/poor assessment of risks
   - What are this young person's peer relationships and how does he/she respond to peer pressure? To what extent is this young person's delinquency driven by a need for peer approval? What alternative ways to gain recognition did this young person see?

- What is this young person good at and how recognized is he/she for this ability?
- Does this young person have an immature identity?
- Does this young person have immature moral reasoning? For whom does he/she show empathy? What is his/her understanding of fairness, rights, responsibility and loyalty?
- To whom is this young person most attached? What is the young person's sense of belonging to family?
- To the extent it can be determined, at the time of the offense, to what extent was this young person able to anticipate? Reacting to threat? Minimizing danger? Seeing only one choice? Able to plan? Influenced by peers?

For criminal defense-based social work, the risk and protective factors present in a client's early and middle childhood and adolescence, based on areas of inquiry earlier, begin to tell a story about the client's life and how he or she become more susceptible to involvement in the juvenile or adult criminal justice system. Generally, a culmination of risk factors, and likely a deficiency of protective factors during crucial periods of development, contribute to a greater likelihood of involvement in the criminal justice system (Youth.gov, n.d.).

In looking at Rodrigo's life history again, he experienced numerous risk factors from an early age, including abuse and neglect by his biological parents; separation from his sibling at only 3 years; early and consistent involvement in the child welfare system; and exposure to drug use, neglect, and physical abuse by one of his first foster families. In contrast, let's revisit Ben's case and life history. While Ben certainly experienced risk factors throughout his life, unlike Rodrigo, he had a culmination of risk factors in middle childhood and adolescence and fewer in early childhood. Although Ben's father was gang involved, Ben lived in a relatively stable home environment. He experienced poverty and community violence but had the protective factors of a stable home life to balance the chaos. However, when Ben was 10 years old, his parents divorced, and the risk factors compounded. By age 14, he was jumped into the Bloods gang. After age 14, his exposure to trauma and violence drastically increased. Gang involvement is an extraordinary risk factor for adolescents because it exposes them to interpersonal and community violence, and is often a deterrent to pro-social involvement or protective factors like family, school, extracurricular activities, etc. that can buffer or minimize such risk factors (Klein, 1995; Thornberry, 1998). Moreover, gang membership often occurs at a time when teenagers are extremely susceptible to peer pressure and lacking the cognitive maturity to think about the consequences of their or their peers' actions (Amicus Curiae brief in Miller v. Alabama and Jackson v. Hobbs, 2009, p. 26; Battin-Pearson, Thornberry, Hawkins, & Krohn, 1998).

In the cases of both Rodrigo and Ben, the unique timing and presentation of risk and protective factors, as well as the individual experiences of trauma while at different stages of development, impacted them differently. The forensic social worker on each case will need to understand and develop the risk factors, protective factors, and experiences of trauma surrounding each client and how that may have led to their current involvement in the criminal justice system. Additionally, the forensic social worker will need to plan for ways to increase the protective factors and decrease current or future risk factors, if reentry or community sentencing is an option.

Identification and Evaluation of Criminogenic Needs

When reviewing and analyzing a client's life history, it is important to understand what life events or experiences increased their susceptibility to criminal involvement. In addition to identifying risk and protective factors, administering the ACE Study, and completing a developmental assessment with the client, the forensic social worker can identify past, present, and future criminogenic needs to better assess why he or she was involved in unlawful behavior and recommend treatment that will promote rehabilitation and not recidivism in the future. When a forensic social worker evaluates a client's life for criminogenic needs, there are four major and moderate factors to consider. The "big four" are proposed to be the major predictors in the analysis of criminal behavior of individuals. These include criminal history, antisocial personality pattern, antisocial cognition, and antisocial associates (Bonta & Andrews, 2007). The "moderate four" are family/marital circumstances, school/work, leisure/recreation, and substance use. The "moderate four" can also be protective factors that are developed more easily and effectively in the community and help protect against future criminal involvement. When suggesting treatment options for a client, the forensic social worker should consider the client's "moderate four" criminogenic needs and make sure to promote recommendations that align with those protective factors already in place and those that can be strengthened. According to the Risk-Need-Responsivity model, an individual's level of recidivism should correspond with the intensity of treatment. In other words, a higher recidivism risk requires a more intensive intervention, whereas a lower recidivism risk requires a less-intensive intervention for positive outcomes. Thus, it becomes important to weigh the "big four" and the "moderate four" against each other to decide how long someone will benefit in treatment before he or she becomes higher risk due to the separation from his or her community and other protective factors. Treatment should reduce the prevalence of the "big four," like antisocial cognitions and associates, but if treatment is too long and becomes unnecessary, it may inadvertently weaken the "moderate four" thereby increasing, not reducing, the individual's recidivism risk by weakening the protective factors that individual has (Bonta & Andrews, 2007) (Table 4.1).

TABLE 4.1 Criminogenic Needs Chart

Criminogenic needs	*Protective factors*	*Risk factors*
Criminal history Early and past involvement with illegal activities		
Antisocial personality Impulsive, pleasure-seeking, and show disregard for others		
Antisocial cognition Negative attitudes, beliefs, and values toward the law; justify criminal behavior		
Antisocial peers/associates Relationships with other criminally involved individuals		

Created by Ezra Aldern, LCSW, used with permission.

Work Product

A forensic social worker develops various forms of work product including written reports, visual demonstratives, and oral presentations. The details of work product will be covered in depth in Chapter 6, "Work Product."

Skill Building

While not therapists, supporting clients in development of skills is a part of the forensic social worker's role on the criminal defense team. It is beneficial to the client, the client's case, and the community at large to help clients develop or strengthen certain skills to improve current functioning and/or readiness for treatment. These skills might include understanding the effects of trauma, disabilities, and immaturity on their behavior; developing mindfulness; anger management; cognitive-behavioral modification; conflict resolution; and basic daily skills. Many young people begin the process of change after their arrest and in detention or jail because of the self-understanding that their forensic social worker guides them toward. This can be rooted in motivational interviewing (Miller & Rollnick, 2002) which the forensic social worker can utilize to prepare the client for change.

Education

Psychoeducation is another important skill for the forensic social worker who provides practical information to the client and family, criminal defense team, and the judicial system. Psychoeducation refers to "...the process of providing education and information to those seeking or receiving mental health services..." (Goodtherapy.org). The forensic social worker is in the best position to explain the client's symptoms, and educate the client, family, defense team, and the court about a multitude of variables that may be impacting the client including maturity, disabilities, trauma, mental illness, substance use and abuse, trauma-informed care, developmental delays, traumatic brain injury, and evidence-based treatment options, among many others.

Termination

Lastly, any social worker must have the clinical skills related to termination. Specifically, when the legal case is over, the forensic social worker must become skilled at thoughtfully and appropriately ending the supportive relationship that was built with the client. Termination should be discussed at the outset of their work together. Depending upon the agency, the criminal defense-based forensic social worker usually terminates with a client when the legal case has ended. A client must understand that termination will occur from the start and together the forensic social worker and the client slowly prepare for the impending termination as the legal case is ending. Effective termination includes coming to a mutually agreed upon end to the professional and client relationship. In criminal defense-based social work, this is often when the client is sentenced. Grodzki (2000) defines positive termination by noting that "full support in leaving translates to educating your clients about their role in making a good ending and then doing your part – helping them to leave with an absence of guilt or shame" (p. 130). By talking about the goals of termination from the onset, a good ending can be accomplished.

Teamwork and Collaboration

Criminal defense-based social workers are on legal defense teams with attorneys, investigators, and paralegals. Thus, strong skills related to teamwork, effective collaboration, and conflict resolution are imperative. Additionally, collaboration with state agencies, such as detention facilities, jails, prisons, Departments of Human Services, and local schools, is paramount to collecting necessary documents, building support systems, and gaining resources for your client.

Barriers

There may be many barriers to working effectively as a criminal defense-based forensic social worker. First, not all the professionals are on the defense side. For example, forensic social workers are often asked to present mitigation information to the district attorney who is prosecuting the case against a client.

Moreover, the position of forensic social worker is not well known to other professionals in most criminal justice or mental health systems. Clients are often housed in a detention facility or prison. Some courtrooms, judges, attorneys, and facility staff have never encountered a criminal defense-based forensic social worker. Members of your own team may have never worked alongside a forensic social worker. Additionally, the client and his or her family do not know what a forensic social worker is, or they may have had a negative experience with a different kind of social worker in the past. Any one of these barriers can be overcome through appropriate training and exchanges of information.

Restorative Justice Opportunity

The opportunity for restorative justice can arise in some criminal justice agencies. Restorative justice practices give crime victims the opportunity to express the full impact of the crime on themselves and their families, ask and get answers to any lingering questions about what occurred, and participate in holding the offender accountable for his or her actions. Many defendants also seek opportunities to apologize to their victims and/or the loved ones of their victim(s). They often do not get the opportunity to do so because the criminal justice system can be divisive. Restorative justice, when executed correctly, can be a powerful tool for healing for all involved.

There are some important considerations, including the type of crime involved, if the defense or victim initiates the contact, if the forensic social worker will be involved, or if an outside organization will facilitate the communication. Defense-Initiated Victim Outreach (DIVO) seeks to address the needs of crime victims and their families throughout the legal process by providing a bridge between the victim-survivors and the defendant through dialogue initially between a victim outreach specialist and the attorneys who represent the defendant. Although this process is initiated by the defense, it is victim-centered (Defense-Initiated Victim Outreach, n.d.; Institute for Restorative Justice and Restorative Dialogue, 2009). Victim outreach will be discussed more thoroughly in Chapter 7, "Forensic Social Work and Collaboration with Expert Witnesses."

Practical Skills

Assessing Mental Health, Substance Abuse, Developmental Disabilities, and Head Trauma

Many criminal defendants have the same mental health, substance abuse, developmental disabilities, and head trauma issues as other social work client populations. Criminal defense-based social workers should be well versed in many of the same practical skills as other social workers. Upon meeting with a new client, the forensic social worker may or may not have some background information. Regardless is it still important to assess a client's mental health symptoms, history of treatment (particularly trauma treatment), medication, and family history to appropriately advocate for treatment. Intellectual and developmental disabilities may be obvious when first meeting with a client or may be deduced over time. The same goes for a history of head trauma. A history of head trauma is not always known or documented in records, but the social worker may suspect or learn about head injuries and changes to the client's behavior, mood, etc. from the client and his or her family. The documentation and previous history of mental health, substance abuse treatment, developmental disabilities, and head trauma may not be correct. Seeking or creating a current, up-to-date assessment may be an important part of the forensic social worker's role and skill set. This will be further discussed in Chapter 6, "Work Product."

Take a closer look at the case study of Deb. Deb's medical and school records have documented a great deal of information regarding her developmental disability and will be important resources for the forensic social worker. Deb's IQ was first tested when she entered public school as a kindergartner. It was then determined that she had an IQ of 68 and she remained in special education classes throughout her academic life. Medical records also confirm that Deb was slow to meet her developmental milestones, and hospital records confirm her report of sexual abuse when she was 8 years old. The forensic social worker does not have the records from treatment but is told by Deb and her mother that she saw a therapist weekly for 2 years after being sexually abused.

While the forensic social worker smells alcohol on her mother during the first visit and the attorney expresses concern over mom's alcoholism, there is minimal mention of this in the medical records or school records. To further assess Deb's current functioning and well-being in her mother's home, the forensic social worker would like to talk further with Deb about her mother's drinking. Even though there is record of Deb's IQ being tested, her adaptive skills have never been tested. The forensic social worker may encourage the attorney to find an expert to test her adaptive skills in conjunction with a current IQ test.

With Deb's written permission, the forensic social worker would also like to speak with Deb's mom and request the treatment records from the therapist she saw at age 8. Deb held a job for 5 years; thus, speaking with her former boss about why she lost her job, how she was as an employee, and if there is an option to return to work may be beneficial. Collecting this additional information would help assess her current functioning in the context of her developmental disability and her mother's alcohol abuse.

Crisis Intervention

Crisis intervention is a potentially life-saving skill in almost every realm of social work practice. According to Hepworth et al. (2002), crisis intervention is a general intervention that is time-limited and "focuses on problems of living rather than psychopathology" (p. 382). A client's safety and the safety of the community in relation to the client are hallmarks of the National Association of Social Worker (NASW)'s Code of Ethics. Social workers in all areas of practice are trained to respond to reports of suicidal ideations, homicidal ideations, and abuse. Crisis intervention as a forensic social worker may be more complicated than in other areas of social work. As a member of the defense team, the forensic social worker is tasked with balancing his or her own code of ethics with the ethics of the defense attorney, agency policies, and mandatory reporting laws of the state in which he or she works. The complexities of crisis intervention as a criminal defense-based social worker were discussed earlier in Chapter 2, "Guiding Principles of Practice".

Incorporating Current Research

To provide effective mitigation for each client, a criminal defense-based forensic social worker must have a wide range of academic knowledge. In addition to social work training, this base of knowledge includes criminology, sociology, psychological theories, child development, risk and protective factors, trauma-informed care, and various evidence-based treatment models. Having a strong understanding of current social sciences research will help in working with the client, developing strong mitigation, and identifying appropriate treatment resources.

Community Resources, Referrals, and Reentry

Criminal defense-based forensic social workers develop a knowledge of available community resources for a client while he or she is incarcerated, upon reentry and as alternatives to sentencing. One of the skills of the criminal defense-based social worker is the ability to translate this clinical information, including the importance of treatment into common language that defense attorneys, district attorneys, and those in the judicial system understand and value. A forensic social worker can translate clinical information into concepts that a diverse group of professionals will understand by explaining its value from varying perspectives, including financial, health, humanistic, and mitigation. For example, a financial perspective might include the cost versus benefit analysis of an alternative day treatment center compared to a sentence of 6 months of incarceration. The forensic social worker would also explain how the treatment received might decrease a client's recidivism which would also address the humanistic perspective in treating the client's mental health issues. Another example might include explaining a client's health struggles detailed in the life history in hopes of mitigating the potential sentencing range and asking for a lesser sentence.

Identification of community resources is critical. Community resources might be as simple as referring a client to the local mental health center that has an immediate appointment available. On the other hand, it may be as complex as teaching the client the public transportation system, securing bus tokens, finding out the times for a walk-in therapy or medication management appointment, finding housing resources, or helping your client to understand terms of probation. Resources, referrals, and reentry plans are never easy, but there are many ways to tackle this skill of a criminal defense-based forensic social worker (more about reentry plans and an example in Chapter 6, "Work Product").

Keep in mind that while there are specific themes present in many cases, each client, case, and dynamic is different. This is often a need for the defense team to be creative. Each agency or individual social worker may keep a database of available resources in the community. Be familiar with what is available in the community as well as any gaps or lapses in treatment resources. It is important to consider whether a database of community resources exists and if so, how it is updated. Identifying community resources can be difficult and time-consuming. It is often beneficial to collaborate with other social workers and team members. It is wise to tour different community agencies in person to meet the staff and clientele. This will help the forensic social worker understand what is offered, what client might be a good fit, and form a working relationship with some of the resources in the community. Experiencing a treatment facility firsthand can also help a forensic social worker better advocate for or against that treatment option for a client. If a forensic social worker has firsthand experience or familiarity with a treatment center or other community resource, he or she can explain to the Court or to district attorneys in a report why it is or is not an appropriate resource for the client.

Unfortunately, many factors may contribute to a forensic social worker being unable to find appropriate referrals, resources, and reentry services. Location (i.e., a rural community), financial funding, political climate, and high demand (i.e., wait-lists) are major barriers. For example, the case study of Ben presents several barriers specific to mental health treatment. Ben has been in jail for about 2 months without adequate mental health services to treat his symptoms of anxiety and possibly depression. In general, jails are not designed to treat individuals with mental illness in the least restrictive or most clinically effective manner. A forensic social worker may utilize his or her skills to advocate for Ben, teach Ben to advocate for himself and secure what services are available.

Ben is in the midst of anxiety and emotional disruption. Once he trusts the social worker, he or she can assist Ben in filling out a request to be seen by medical or a psychiatrist at the jail. While Ben waits to be seen, the forensic social worker can see him on a more frequent basis to support him emotionally, assess his mental health, and help him learn about the sources of his anxiety. There is often a wait-list to be seen in a jail, so the forensic social worker would be wise to form a working relationship with the medical staff at the jail if possible. Once Ben begins taking psychiatric medication at the jail and becomes more stabilized, it may be beneficial for an outside therapist to come into the jail weekly and work with Ben. This will take some research into resources and connecting of professionals by the forensic social worker.

Practical Tips

Community resources for the forensic population upon reentry can often be frustrating. Available resources can vary by state, political climate, socioeconomic level, and urban/rural/suburban community. There is no one right way to expand upon reentry services. It takes perseverance and often creativity. The following is a list of methods to learn about, collect, and expand upon services in the community.

- Keep a list of what is available and update contact information quarterly
- Schedule tours of jails, prisons, mental health centers, substance abuse centers, and homeless facilities
- Keep a list of contacts for services and networking purposes
- Connect with other forensic social workers and meet quarterly
- Keep a list of what services are lacking and what is needed
- Reach out to local legislator
- Reach out to a client's family members
- Attend conferences to learn how other communities are serving their forensic population
- Start your own nonprofit
- Get creative!

Conclusion

While many of the traditional skills of a social worker overlap with the skills of a criminal defense-based forensic social worker, such as building rapport, crisis intervention, clinical assessment, skill building, psychoeducation, records review, and report writing, there are multiple skills unique to this growing field of social work. Motivational interviewing, an understanding of the legal system, development of mitigation, team collaboration, incorporation of current research, identification of reentry services, and an understanding of criminogenic needs are unique to this type of forensic social work and an important part of the field. While the field of forensic social work is exciting and evolving, solid social work skills will build a stronger foundation for future criminal defense-based forensic social workers.

References

American Psychological Association. (2009). Amici Curiae brief in Miller v. Alabama and Jackson v. Hobbs, 1–35.

Baglivio, M., Epps, N., Schwartz, K., Huq, M., Sheer, A., & Hardt, N. (2014). The prevalence of adverse childhood experiences (ACE) in the lives of juvenile offenders. *Journal of Juvenile Justice, 3*(2), 1–107.

Battin-Pearson, S.R., Thornberry, T., Hakinds, J.D., & Krohn, M. (1998). Gang membership, delinquent peers, and delinquent behavior. *Juvenile Justice Bulletin*, 1–12.

Bonta, J., & Andrews, D. (2007). *Risk-need-responsivity model for offender assessment and rehabilitation* (Report no. 2007–06). Ottawa, Canada: Department of Public Safety and Emergency Preparedness Canada.

Coie, J.D., Watt, N.F., West, S.G., Hawkins, J.D., Asarnow, J.R., Markman, H.J., Long, B. (1993). The science of prevention: A conceptual framework and some directions for a national research program. *American Psychologist, 48*(10), 1013–1022.

Defense-Initiated Victim Outreach. (n.d.). Retrieved March 1, 2018, from https://divo.irjrd.org

Felitti, V.J., Anda, R.F., Nordenberg, D., Williamson, D.F., Spitz, A.M., Edwards, V., … Marks, J.S. (2014, May 13). *The Adverse Childhood Experiences (ACE) study.* Retrieved November 25, 2017, from http://www.cdc.gov/violenceprevention/acestudy/index.html

Ford, J.D., Chapman, J.F., Hawke, J., & Albert, D. (2007). *Trauma among youth in the juvenile justice system: Critical issues and new directions.* National Center for Mental Health and Juvenile Justice. 6/2007. Retrieved January 24, 2018, from https://www.ncmhjj.com

Grodzki, L. (2000). *Building your ideal private practice.* New York, NY: W.W. Norton & Company.

Hepworth, D.H., Rooney, R.H., & Larson, J.A. (2002). *Direct social work practice.* New York, NY: Thomas Learning.

Herrenkohl, T.L., Maguin, E., Hill, K.G., Hawkins, J.D., Abbott, R.D., & Catalano, R.F. (2000). Developmental risk factors for youth violence. *Journal of Adolescent Health, 26*(7), 176–186.

Institute for Restorative Justice and Restorative Dialogue. (2009). *Defense-initiated victim outreach master manual.* Retrieved March 9, 2018, from https://divo.irjrd.org/files/2016/04/master-manual.pdf

Kadushin, A., & Kadushin, G. (2012). *The social worker interview: A guide for human service professionals* (4th ed.). New York, NY: Columbia University.

Klein, M.W. (1995). *The American street gang: Its nature, prevalence, and control.* New York, NY: Oxford University Press.

Miller, W.R., & Rollnick, S. (2002). *Motivational interviewing: Preparing people for change* (2nd ed.). New York, NY: The Guillford Press.

Office of the Surgeon General. (2001). *Youth violence: A report of the Surgeon General.* Retrieved from January 1, 2018, from https://www.surgeongeneral.gov/library/youthviolence/toc.html

Youth.gov. (n.d.). *Risk and protective factors.* Youth.gov. Retrieved January 1, 2018, from https://youth.gov/youth-topics/juvenile-justice/risk-and-protective-factors

Thornberry, T. (1998). Membership in youth gangs and involvement in serious and violent offending. In R. Loeber & D.P. Farrington (Eds.), *Serious & violent juvenile offenders: Risk factors and successful interventions.* Thousand Oaks, CA: Sage Publications, Inc.

5

CULTURAL HUMILITY AND SPECIAL POPULATIONS

Claire Schmidt and Molly Hennessey

Abstract

This chapter examines the importance of cultural humility within forensic social work. Forensic social workers come into contact with individuals with diverse cultural and social backgrounds. Forensic social workers must be able to investigate and articulate the client's experience and strengths, which exist as a result of the client's complex cultural identity and perspective. Cultural humility will be defined in this chapter and expanded upon. In addition, this chapter will highlight examples of special populations found within the criminal justice system.

Learning Objectives

- Understand the definition and importance of cultural humility versus cultural competence
- Identify and understand various special populations found within the criminal and juvenile justice population
- Identify how forensic social workers can investigate, gather information, and present the client's story in a way that honors and highlights their unique identity, perspective, culture, and voice
- Examine the case study to examine how the client's cultural identity, experiences, and family background can be beneficial to developing their social history

As social workers, we are responsible for recognizing and honoring every client's unique cultural identity. The United States is a diverse country growing every day and there are many forms of diversity. Most commonly, diversity is thought of in terms of racial, socioeconomic, ethnic, gender, or geographic differences. However, diversity also includes but is not limited to differences in academic or professional backgrounds, disability, religious beliefs, political beliefs, sexual orientation, and life experiences. The many forms of diversity and their intersectionality impact and create one's cultural identity and perspective. Intersectionality, a term coined by Critical Race Theory scholar Kimberle Williams Crenshaw, refers to the presence of overlapping identities that come together to create one's social and cultural identity (Crenshaw, 1989). Overlapping identities are not mutually exclusive. For example, a woman who identifies as Native American and Lesbian has experiences from moving in the world as a Native American person, as a woman, and as a Lesbian, respectively; however, we would be remiss to discount the unique experience of navigating the world as a Native American, Lesbian woman. In recognizing intersectionality in our client's cultural identity, we are able to unpack a more comprehensive picture of an individual's overall experiences, needs, and strengths.

Definition of Terms—Cultural Humility and Special Populations

As forensic social workers, we choose to use the phrase cultural humility rather than cultural competency. This choice is intentional because the term cultural competency implies an arrival at or achievement of mastery regarding the many cultural identities and perspectives of those with whom we work. The term cultural humility better describes the process-oriented approach of being open to and honoring an individual's cultural identity. Hook, Davis, Owen, Worthington and Utsey (2013) conceptualize cultural humility as the "ability to maintain an interpersonal stance that is other-oriented (or open to the other) in relation to aspects of cultural identity that are most important to the client" (p. 2). It is imperative for forensic social workers to incorporate and strive toward cultural humility in their practice.

Just as the general population of the United States is growing in diversity and multiculturalism, so is the population of individuals coming into contact with the criminal justice system. However, there are stark disparities and an overrepresentation of people of color, the poor, and other disenfranchised populations in the criminal justice system in comparison to the demographics of the general public. The racial disparities in the criminal justice system are seen at every step of the process, including, but not limited to, disproportioned contact with police and law enforcement, disproportionate rates of filings of charges, disparate treatment in whether courts grant a person a bond while awaiting trial, and significantly disproportionate rates of incarceration (The Sentencing Project, 2016).

The National Association for the Advancement of Colored People (NAACP) notes that that while the United States is only 5% of the world's population, it has 21% of the world's prison population. Within this population, there are vast racial disparities in the juveniles and adults incarcerated. Human Rights Watch reports that black men are incarcerated at six times the rate of white men. The American Civil Liberties Union (ACLU) reports that one in three African American men are incarcerated in their lifetime, compared to one in six Latino males and one in 17 Caucasian males. African American women are incarcerated at twice the rate of Caucasian women (NAACP, n.d.). In regard to youth and young adults in the juvenile justice system, children of color represent 32% of those arrested, 42% of detained children, and 52% of children charged in adult court (NAACP, n.d.).

Racial bias, unjust and outdated laws, and biased policing continue to contribute to these issues and the overrepresentation of minority groups in our legal system. It is part of the ethical duty of the forensic social worker to identify and work to address these disparities. As social workers, we often interface and engage with members of marginalized populations while at the same time looking like or having characteristics of the systems or individuals who have marginalized them. These characteristics can include race, gender, socioeconomic status, profession, and/or level of education. This requires social workers to strive toward a more critical consciousness of the many forms of our own power and privilege while working toward the recognition and validation of the cultural identity and experiences of others.

The lesbian, gay, bisexual, transgender, and queer or questioning (LGBTQ+) community is another example of a group that is also overrepresented within our juvenile and criminal justice systems. A national study found that while 3.8% of adults identify as LGBT, 7.9% of adults in prison identify as LGBT, and 7.1% of adults in jails identify as LGBT (CAP & MAP, 2016). In juvenile detention facilities, 20% of youth identify as LGBT, compared to 7%–9% of youth in the United States who identify as LGBT (CAP & MAP, 2016). The LGBT community often faces challenges that increase their likelihood of interfacing with the criminal justice system, such as homelessness and increased risk of rejection and victimization by family or friends.

In addition to the groups discussed earlier, there are many other groups and clients who are marginalized because of their identities or membership in other special populations. These individuals have unique needs and strengths as a result. There is expansive research dedicated to diving into a more thorough exploration of other cultural, social, ethnic, or racial identities that can impact a person's perspective. However, within the scope of this chapter, we are not able to capture all pertinent information but rather offer examples and considerations. Exploring each client's individual intersectionality is imperative in the role of forensic social worker.

Forensic Social Workers Challenge Social Justice

Working to maintain cultural humility allows forensic social workers to develop a more comprehensive approach to identifying mitigation opportunities and resources as well as fostering strong relationships with the client and a client's support system in order to best advocate for clients within the criminal justice system. There is an inherent difference in how forensic social workers view their clients and how the criminal justice system is designed to view and treat clients. The criminal justice system is structured to view all who come before it as "equal" or "the same" under the law. The Declaration of Independence's famous clause mandating that "all men are created equal under the law" highlights this inherent intended value. However, this intention and the daily reality of those who experience the criminal justice system are often very different.

The criminal justice system is largely a punitive system focusing on the alleged crime that was committed. Forensic social workers are uniquely situated to not only assist defense counsel but also to assist decision-makers around the individual person and lay out clearly developmental considerations together with the various intersecting identities each unique client holds. Forensic social workers are tasked with highlighting and presenting pertinent information including various aspects of an individual's identity or experience that contribute to their overall functioning. Forensic social workers must show the uniqueness of each client through their work. This can mean highlighting experiences of trauma, marginalization, age, disability, or immigration status to show that all that who enter the criminal justice are not the "same" and often do not experience "equal" privilege in American society. This apparent value contradiction is the space in which forensic social workers practice. Therefore, practicing cultural humility is one of the most powerful tools in a forensic social worker's tool kit.

Special Populations Overview

The term special population is typically used to describe a group of individuals that experiences oppression or who are disadvantaged in comparison to the general population. This disadvantage or oppression can be a result of society's lack of acceptance or be because of limitations due to disability or illness. Cultural humility is imperative when working with members of special populations. The concept of cultural humility allows the forensic social worker to approach their work with every client, especially those who identify or are identified as members of a special population, from an open perspective in order to genuinely seek to understand each individual's experience. Individuals, who have disabilities, are suffering from mental illness, are economically disadvantaged, are ethnic or racial minorities, and who identify as LGBTQ are all examples of members of special populations. One of the greatest skills that forensic social workers bring to defense teams is their ability to provide context to how a client's membership in a special population may impact or contribute to the client's involvement in the criminal justice system. This includes evaluating collateral records and interviews to highlight the historical presence of disability or mental illness, as well as identifying the effects of being devalued by society as some members of special populations experience.

Special Population: Juveniles and Juveniles Serving Life Without Parole

Juveniles are an especially vulnerable population within the criminal justice system due to their age, developmental stage, lack of maturity, and susceptibility to outside influences.

The first juvenile court in the United States was established in 1899 in Cook County, Illinois (McCord, Widom, & Cromwell, 2001). Many states soon followed suit, and now juvenile courts operate across the entire country, although how juvenile courts are run varies state by state and even county by county. It was formerly widely accepted in the criminal justice system that children differ from adults and thus should be treated differently and with a more rehabilitative approach. Following a crime wave in the 1990s, many states passed extremely harsh and punitive legislation to combat juvenile crime (McCord, Widom, & Cromwell, 2001). Many states now have legislation where children are automatically charged as adults depending on age and the crime committed, which will be discussed further below. In addition to criminal charges, juvenile courts also deal with status offenses. Status offenses are charges that only apply to underage juveniles, such as truancy, running away, behavioral issues that do not result in delinquency charges, minors in possession of alcohol, or curfew violations. Many juveniles involved with the juvenile system also have involvement with other systems, such as the child welfare system.

When working with juveniles or individuals serving life without parole as a result of an incident that happened when they were juveniles, forensic social workers need to be conscious of their client's development, both in the context of normative adolescence, as well as any potential development concerns or deficits. Recent studies have indicated that the human brain continues to grow in structure and function at least through the twenties, suggesting that all juvenile clients lack a fully developed prefrontal cortex, which limits their ability to make decisions, particularly in high-risk or peer-involved situations (Albert, Chein, & Steinberg, 2013). Furthermore, young clients who have faced adversity are likely to also have social, psychological, and biological delays and deficits. Social science and developmental research can not only inform the team on possible mitigation themes but can also help the legal team to work effectively with their client.

Juveniles charged in adult court and juveniles serving life without parole for crimes committed when under the age of 18 are a particularly vulnerable population within the system. The overarching characteristic of youth contributes to an individual's vulnerability, capacity for change, and overall level of functioning. While youth should not be considered a disadvantage or disability, it must be considered and addressed when seeking fair and proper representation, intervention, and determination of culpability and sentencing. Juveniles are fundamentally different than adults in their cognitive, physiological, and emotional functioning. Forensic social workers can assist defense teams in highlighting unique factors the court and district attorneys must take into consideration when charging juveniles with crimes in adult court.

Many states have different ways in which a juvenile may be prosecuted in adult court. As of 2017, 13 states have direct file laws (Sago, 2017). Between 1985 and 2017, the number of states with direct file laws doubled (Sago, 2017). Most states have statutory factors for consideration within the determination of jurisdiction: Juvenile court or adult court consistent with the seminal case *Kent v. United States*, 383 U.S. 541 (1966). For purposes of this chapter, the focus will be upon the law in Colorado and the important work forensic social workers are able to do to best support a defense team working toward a transfer hearing or reverse-transfer hearing.

In Colorado, district attorneys have discretion in whether to charge juveniles 16 years of age and older who are accused of certain criminal charges in the adult criminal justice system, according to Colorado Revised Statutes Title 19 Children's Code §19-2-517. This action is called direct file. When a juvenile is direct filed, the district attorney is asking the court to view that young person as an adult for all future court proceedings, including the sentencing phase, which for many juveniles means lengthy prison terms in adult correctional facilities. Many other states have similar practices. Mandatory sentencing schemes in place for and created for adults are now applied to direct-filed juveniles.

This practice has resulted in many youths in Colorado and across the country now serving mandatory sentences of life without parole, which were imposed upon them for acts committed prior to the age of 18. In 2012, the United States Supreme Court declared mandatory life without parole unconstitutional and required an individualized look at the youth with certain factors for consideration as a result of the *Miller v. Alabama*, 132 S. Ct. 2455 (2012). This case prompted legislation across the country for these offenders to be resentenced, and in many instances, including in Colorado, the court must consider a list of factors consistent with the *Miller* decision. Many of these juveniles who are now adults have spent decades in prison for the crimes they committed in their youth and this aspect will also be part of their story toward resentencing.

Forensic social workers play an instrumental and critical role in helping defense teams prepare for transfer hearings, reverse-transfer hearings, and resentencing hearings for juveniles serving life without parole. Forensic social workers can help teams prepare mitigation presenting the impacts that trauma and membership in a special population can have on an individual, as well as outline important factors regarding adolescent brain development. Relevant research regarding brain development validates that juveniles are different than adults, most notably in decision-making and level of maturity. This is very relevant when determining the question of culpability and amenability for change or rehabilitation in the context of the criminal justice system. In Colorado, there are 12 factors that a judge must consider when ruling in a reverse-transfer hearing to determine if a juvenile will be charged in adult or juvenile court. States across the country additionally have identified similar factors used to determine whether a juvenile case will be transferred into adult court or remain in juvenile court. The following three factors are especially relevant for a forensic social worker's work with the young person, their family, and friends, and should be the guiding force in the record review and work product created to help the defense team argue for the juvenile to remain in juvenile court.

> (IV) THE AGE OF THE JUVENILE AND THE MATURITY OF THE JUVENILE AS DETERMINED BY CONSIDERATIONS OF THE JUVENILE'S HOME, ENVIRONMENT, EMOTIONAL ATTITUDE, AND PATTERN OF LIVING
>
> (VI) THE CURRENT AND PAST MENTAL HEALTH STATUS OF THE JUVENILE AS EVIDENCED BY RELEVANT MENTAL HEALTH OR PSYCHOLOGICAL ASSESSMENTS OR SCREENINGS THAT ARE MADE AVAILABLE TO BOTH THE DISTRICT ATTORNEY AND DEFENSE COUNSEL
>
> (VII) THE LIKELIHOOD OF THE JUVENILE'S REHABILITATION BY USE OF THE SENTENCING OPTIONS AVAILABLE IN THE JUVENILE COURTS AND 4 DISTRICT COURTS

These factors indicate that a juvenile's social history, developmental considerations, and mental health are relevant when determining their fate in the criminal justice system. Interviewing and record review are two important tools for developing information to support an argument that a juvenile's best chance for intervention, rehabilitation, and low future recidivism lie within the juvenile justice system rather than the adult criminal justice system. Creating a thorough developmental assessment can be invaluable for the defense team and critical to understanding an individual, their culture, and how they may intersect. Information on how to prepare a developmental assessment will be discussed further in Chapter 4, "Skills."

Special Population—Individuals with Disabilities

Individuals living with a disability are also considered to be a special population. The Americans with Disabilities Act (ADA) became law in 1990 and defines a person with a disability as someone who has a physical or mental impairment that significantly limits one or more major life activity. There are many different types and severities of disabilities. Forensic social workers often work with people with long-standing identified disabilities but also interface with individuals who struggle with unidentified disabilities. It is not usual for forensic social workers to be the first professionals to identify developmental, cognitive, or learning disabilities when observing and evaluating a client's overall functioning. When forensic social workers are observing a client's struggle with processing or comprehending information, it is a cue that an external expert such as a psychologist or neuropsychologist might be necessary to fully understand that client's level of functioning.

The identification of language impairment concerns and auditory processing disorders are examples of disorders that can be particularly notable when exploring a juvenile client's lack of involvement or achievement in education. Auditory processing disorder refers to a child who can hear words but processes the sounds in an atypical manner. However, a language impairment disorder refers to one's ability to attach meaning and create a meaningful response (Sharma, Purdy, & Kelly, 2009). These disorders affect the way a child interacts with their surroundings and they can become a more passive observer in social or learning environments. Understanding these disorders and how they are different can also be helpful to forensic social workers while evaluating Individualized Education Programs (IEPs) or advocating for appropriate school-based interventions.

There are four federally recognized categories for youth with learning differences: Emotionally disturbed, developmentally handicapped, learning disabled, and behaviorally handicapped (Mallett, 2009). Research focusing on the prevalence of youth in the juvenile justice system who have special education needs has found that youth with learning differences and disabilities make up between 33% and 41% of those in juvenile detention facilities (Mallett, 2009). A study examining the relationship between youth with disabilities and outcomes of juvenile probation found that youth who were receiving various services for their educational disability not only were less successful while on probation but also had higher rates of incarceration (Mallett, 2009). The identification of learning differences, connection to appropriate resources, advocacy in the educational system, and an understanding of the impact of a youth's specific learning difference are all fundamental to comprehensive representation in the legal system. A youth's disability may impact their behavior as well as their ability to comprehend and assist their legal team, communicate their needs, and function in their environment. The forensic social worker is an important advocate for the client. Early identification or determination of disability is critical as it can inform how the legal team can best meet their client's needs in addition to informing potential mitigation themes.

Special Population: Competency and Mental Health

The question of competency may also arise for a person who struggles with a significant intellectual or developmental disability, physical disorder or severe persistent mental illness. Competence to stand trial is "the legally determined capacity of a criminal defendant to proceed with criminal adjudication" (Mossman et al., 2007, p. 2). While forensic social workers on defense teams do not determine or opine about whether a client is competent, their observations and identification of possible competency issues can be very helpful to a psychologist hired by the state or defense to evaluate an individual's competency to stand trial. Competency and criminal responsibility are distinguished under the law in that a person can be found competent to stand trial and still establish an insanity defense (Mossman et al., 2007).

In order for an individual to be competent to stand trial, he or she must be able to consult with his or her lawyer with a reasonable degree of rational understanding, as well as have a factual understanding of the proceedings against him or her (Roesch, Zapf, Golding, & Skeem, 1999). Forensic social workers are often the members of the defense team who maintain the most frequent, consistent contact with clients. Therefore, observations regarding a client's mental state, comprehension, and overall functioning can be crucial to establishing a clearer picture of the client's overall state. Forensic social workers can create narratives outlining historical information regarding a client's disability gleaned from reviewing records as well information gained from observing or interviewing the client and collateral witnesses. This information can then be synthesized for an outside expert evaluating the client. These narratives can be very helpful to the outside expert because experts often do not have the benefit of spending multiple hours on various occasions with the client or conducting firsthand collateral witness interviews.

Special Population: Military Personnel and Veterans

Individuals who have served in the armed forces, are on active duty, or who are military veterans face many unique challenges upon returning to civilian life. Although recent statistics record a dramatic decrease in the number of incarcerated veterans at the state and federal levels from 2004 to 2012, there are still many veterans who come into contact with the criminal justice system (Bronson, Carson, Noonan, & Bergzofsky, 2015). Due to the unique circumstances and experiences of individuals who have served in the armed forces, it is important to take into consideration and explore the possible factors contributing to their involvement in the criminal justice system. Approximately, half of all veterans in prison and jail have been diagnosed with a mental health disorder (BJS). In addition to the unique challenges many veterans face, the military has a distinct culture and language that often varies from branch to branch. Practicing cultural humility and taking time to learn about a client's experience and perception of his or her individual military experience will provide invaluable information during the social history investigation, which in turn provides invaluable insight for the defense team and attorneys representing the client.

Operation Enduring Freedom (OEF) and Operation Iraqi Freedom (OIF) were the United States' longest sustained military operations since the Vietnam War. However, OIF was very different than other operations undertaken by the United States. In past conflicts, the number of active-duty military personnel was higher than it was for OEF and OIF. Lower numbers of active-duty military personnel in these operations meant that many active-duty service members were being deployed on multiple tours, for longer deployments, and with less time to recover in between deployments than in all previous wars. Repeated and extended deployments created unique challenges and issues for OEF and OIF veterans returning to civilian life after their service concluded. Once home, veterans faced higher rates of unemployment than their non-veteran peers, as well as higher rates of post-traumatic stress disorder (PTSD), traumatic brain injury, depression, and substance abuse (Institute of Medicine, 2010).

Researchers report that 90% of OIF veterans returned home from deployments, which indicates a significantly lower number of fatalities in OEF and OIF than other wars. The lower rate of fatalities was attributed to improvements in medical care, combat evacuation, and body armor provided to soldiers rather than decreased level of exposure to or severity of combat experienced by surviving service members (Institute of Medicine, 2010). This created a challenging dynamic for veterans returning home because, while fortunately many more survived combat, many returned home with severe combat-related issues commonly referred to as "invisible wounds." These invisible wounds include traumatic brain injury and PTSD (Tanielian & Jaycox, 2008).

The moniker "invisible wounds" was coined because although these disorders can cause extreme impairment to overall functioning, they are not as apparent or noticeable as an amputated limb, for example, or other traumatic physical injuries. In fact, traumatic brain injury is considered the most common combat-related injury of OIF (Hoge et al., 2008; Tanielian and Jaycox, 2008) and sustaining a traumatic or mild traumatic brain injury during their most recent deployment is the strongest predictor of post-deployment PTSD for service members (Yurgil et al., 2014). So, while veterans are not currently incarcerated at a higher rate than non-veterans, there are many important factors for a forensic social worker to explore when advocating and creating a mitigation report on behalf of a veteran.

Special Population: Gang Members and Gang Affiliation

Membership in a gang and subsequent delinquent behavior can lead to involvement in the criminal justice system. The National Criminal Justice Service (NCJRS) defines a gang as a group of three or more individuals who engage in criminal activity and identify with a common name or symbol. However, more complex than its definition is the question of why an individual would identify, associate with, or seek membership in a gang. There are many factors and reasons someone might seek out gang involvement. Additionally, there are multiple risk factors associated with a young person joining or associating with a gang.

Individual Risk Factors

- Previous delinquency
- Illegal gun ownership
- Desire for status, companionship, and protection
- Antisocial attitudes
- Aggressive behaviors
- Alcohol and drug use
- Early sexual activity
- Violent victimization.

Peer Group Risk Factors

- Delinquent peers
- Street socialization
- Peers who use drugs
- Peers who are gang involved
- Pre-teen exposure to stress or adverse childhood experiences.

School-Related Risk Factors

- Poor school performance
- Low educational aspirations
- Negative labeling by teachers
- High levels of antisocial behavior
- Disinterest in education
- Low attachment to school
- Learning difficulties.

Family Risk Factors

- Family disorganization, including single-parent homes and parental drug and/or alcohol abuse
- Family violence, neglect, and drug addiction
- Gang membership by family members
- Lack of adult and parental role models, parental criminality, parents with violent attitudes, siblings with antisocial behaviors
- Low socioeconomic status.

Community-Related Risk Factors

- Social disorganization, including high poverty and residential mobility
- High-crime neighborhoods; neighborhood youth in trouble
- Presence of gangs in the neighborhood
- Availability or perceived access to drugs in the neighborhood
- Availability of firearms
- Cultural norms supporting gang behavior
- Feeling unsafe in neighborhood.

Adapted from Howell and Egley (2005), and the National Crime Prevention Centre (2007).

Often, having membership in a gang is a label it can be difficult to separate the client from. Membership in a gang can be a negative way of describing the peers and/or "family" of a client. As a part of developing mitigation, the forensic social worker should seek to identify the psychosocial factors that led the client to membership or affiliation with a gang (Hill, Howell, Hawkins, & Battin-Pearson, 1999). Seeking to understand the cultural identity of gangs and exploring what a client gains from or values about their involvement can provide insight for identifying pro-social interventions or providing context to the court or district attorney about factors that led to a client's gang involvement. Forensic social workers seek to provide context, humanize, and identify possible interventions outside of incarceration for groups society often labels irredeemable or beyond repair. This is especially true for individuals who identify as gang members.

Forensic social workers working with gang-involved clients should also seek to understand the experiences of their clients with gang involvement. Gang members experience a disproportionate amount of violence in comparison to non-gang members (Wu & Pyrooz, 2015), and the forensic social worker should also assess the client with gang involvement for associated trauma and adverse experiences. Affiliation or membership in a gang can bring exposure to violence, crime, and further experiences of trauma.

Case Study

Rodrigo is a 16-year-old male who experienced significant abuse and neglect in the foster care system as a child. He was separated from his brother at the age of 3, and they both grew up moving frequently to different foster homes and assigned to many different therapists and caseworkers. Rodrigo was diagnosed with attention-deficit/hyperactivity disorder (ADHD) when he was 5 years old. Rodrigo is now facing first-degree murder charges in adult court. He says he carries a gun "to protect myself" after an experience with bullying. His biological family lives in Latin America and is Spanish-speaking only.

1. How has Rodrigo's Latino culture impacted him?

Forensic social workers are tasked with spending time learning about how our client's culture, race, and ethnicity impact his or her perspective or worldview.

Although Rodrigo was separated from his biological family at age 3, it is important to understand how Rodrigo identifies with his Latino culture and ethnicity. Rodrigo has expressed that he has sought to understand his heritage and culture as he's grown up in various foster homes with families that did not share his biological family's culture. He reports that he gravitates toward other Latino young men because he feels like he "belongs."

Rodrigo describes a desire to embody behaviors that are commonly known as Machismo. Machismo is a Latino cultural value that is characterized by a strict code and rules for how masculinity should be displayed. Rodrigo has grown to embrace and value traditional strength and masculinity as expressed through limited emotional expression, aggression, and a tough, fearless facade. However, Rodrigo also internalized positive constructs of Machismo also known as Caballerismo, including a strong sense of dignity and responsibility for family and loved ones. (Arciniega, Anderson, Tovar-Blank, & Tracey, 2008).

2. What impact from exposure to trauma affects Rodrigo's life?

It is important for the forensic social worker to record a chronology of physical abuse, sexual abuse, exposure to violence, removal from home and other disrupted caregiving, the loss of a brother and other important individuals, bullying, discrimination, psychological maltreatment, and other life events in any client's history.

Examples of Behaviors and Symptoms of Trauma to Observe and Document

- Slowed development
- Difficulties with self-regulation (easily over-stimulated, limited self-soothing skills, quick to get frustrated)
- Fearfulness, being on constant alert, nightmares, and/or intrusive bad memories

- Numbing feelings and memories with substances
- Trouble concentrating
- Being controlling, especially when anxious
- Unusual irritability
- Depression/suicidal thinking
- Self-protectiveness when feeling threatened (reactive alarm response)
- Mistrusting others
- Difficulty self-calming
- Oversensitive; unusual perception of others as hostile, mean, and/or unfair
- When feelings are hurt, flooded with anger from the past that is of proportion to the present provocation
- Feeling picked on or ostracized
- Self-dislike, self-blaming, and attention-seeking behavior
- Belligerent outspokenness
- Dissociation (unable to remember emotionally charged situations).

3. Does Rodrigo have learning differences?

Observing, identifying, and recording learning problems will be important as the forensic social worker meets with Rodrigo. Additionally, reviewing records and interviewing family members or other important figures in Rodrigo's history can also help support identification of potential learning differences. Chapter 4, "Skills," outlines in detail areas to investigate when identifying and exploring a possible learning problem.

4. How, specifically, does this young person's behavior reflect his/her immature thinking?

As mentioned earlier, evaluating, recording, and demonstrating a juvenile's level of maturity in a Developmental Assessment is a factor that the judge will consider in reverse-transfer hearings. Outlining Rodrigo's immaturity in the context of his exposure to trauma and adolescent brain development is imperative. Questions to consider when evaluating Rodrigo's level of immature thinking can be found within Chapter 4, "Skills."

The basic steps of a social history investigation include interviewing the client, reviewing records, and interviewing other important family members or community members, and are crucial steps for all clients regardless of age. There will be other elements and important factors to consider when developing mitigation reports or demonstratives for clients in other special populations.

Identifying Strengths

Although forensic social workers are often tasked with identifying areas of need, deficits, or challenges their clients face, it is just as important to identify clients' strengths and positive attributes associated with membership in a special population. Using and development of skills such as in-depth interviewing with both the client and their family should reveal a host of positive, adaptive behavior. For example, a person's focus and value of close familial relationships or diligent work ethic should be highlighted in the context of protective factors. Protective factors reduce an individual's risk for adverse outcomes and increase potential for positive outcomes, thus increasing the likelihood for a pro-social future. Forensic social workers must always seek to reveal the full picture of a client's functioning including positive adaptations or areas of resilience. Another example may be a client's discovery and development of other forms of expression such as painting or drawing in the wake of limited formal educational or intellectual limitations. By incorporating a strengths-based assessment of a client, forensic social workers more effectively humanize and advocate for clients within the criminal justice system.

Practical Tips

- Consider the client as the expert of their identity and experiences
- Utilize the Cultural Formulation Interview, available in the Diagnostic and Statistical Manual of Mental Disorders, Fifth Edition (DSM-5)
- Attend training and workshops focusing on different populations and cultural groups
- Utilize supervision and peer consultation to discuss themes in cases
- Use social science and research to learn best practices and interventions

Conclusion

The majority of clients served by forensic social workers have experienced adversity and differential treatment as a result of a number of intersecting cultural identities. Cultural humility is a crucial tenet of forensic social work. Forensic social workers conduct thorough investigations into our clients' backgrounds and cultural identities in order to better understand and advocate for their needs and strengths within the context of the criminal justice system. There are many considerations, skills, and best practices that forensic social workers must maintain and develop in order to serve all clients through the lens of cultural humility.

References

Albert, D., Chein, J., & Steinberg, L. (2013). Peer influences on adolescent decision making. *Current Directions in Psychological Science, 22*(2), 114–120. doi: 10.1177/0963721412471347

Arciniega, G.M., Anderson, T.C., Tovar-Blank, Z.G., & Tracey, T.J. (2008). Toward a fuller conception of Machismo: Development of a traditional Machismo and Caballerismo scale. *Journal of Counseling Psychology, 55*(1), 19.

Bronson, J., Carson, A.E., Noonan, M.E., & Bergzofsky, M. (2015). Veterans in prison and jail 2011. *Bureau of Justice Statistics.* Retrieved from https://www.bjs.gov

Center for American Progress (CAP) & Movement Advancement Project (MAP). (2016). *Unjust: How the broken criminal justice system fails LGBT people.* Retrieved from http://www.lgbtmap.org/file/lgbt-criminal-justice.pdf

Crenshaw, K. (1989). Demarginalizing the intersection of race and sex: A black feminist critique of antidiscrimination doctrine, feminist theory and antiracist politics. *The University of Chicago Legal Forum Volume, 1989*(1), 139.

Hill, K.G., Howell, J.C., Hawkins, J.D., & Battin-Pearson, S. (1999). Childhood risk factors for adolescent gang membership: Results from the Seattle social development project. *Journal of Research in Crime and Delinquency, 6*(3), 300–322. doi: 10.1777/0022327899036003003

Human Rights Watch. (2015). *United States: Events of 2015.* Retrieved from https://www.hrw.org/world-report/2016/country-chapters/united-states#e00bd9

Hoge, C.W., McGurk, D., Thomas, J.L., Cox, A.L., Engel, C.C., & Castro, C.A. (2008). Mild traumatic brain injury in US soldiers returning from Iraq. *New England Journal of Medicine, 358*(5), 453–463.

Hook, J.N., Davis, D.E., Owen, J., Worthington Jr., E.L., & Utsey, S.O. (2013). Cultural humility: Measuring openness to culturally diverse clients. *Journal of Counseling Psychology, 60*(3). doi: 10.1037/a0032595

Howell, J.C. & Egley, A. (2005). Moving risk factors into developmental theories of gang membership. *Youth Violence and Juvenile Justice, 3*(4), 334–354. doi: 101.1177/1541204005278679

Institute of Medicine. (2010). *Returning home from Iraq and Afghanistan: Preliminary assessment of readjustment needs of veterans, service members, and their families.* Washington, DC: The National Academic Press. doi: 10/17226/12812

Kent v. United States, 383 U.S. 541 (1966).

Mallett, C.A. (2009). Disparate juvenile court outcomes for disabled delinquent youth: A social work call to action. *Child and Adolescent Social Work Journal, 26*(3), 197–207. doi: 10.1007/s10560-009-0168-y

McCord, J., Widom, C. S., & Cromwell, N. A. (2001). *Juvenile crime, juvenile justice.* Washington, D.C.: National Academy Press.

Miller v. Alabama. 567 U.S. 460 (2012)

Mossman, D., Noffsinger, S.G., Ash, P., Frierson, R.L., Gerbasi, J., Hackett, M., & Wall, B.W. (2007). AAPL practice guideline for the forensic psychiatric evaluation of competence to stand trial. *Journal of the American Academy of Psychiatry and the Law Online, 35*(Supplement 4), S3–S72.

NAACP. (n.d.). *Criminal justice fact sheet.* Retrieved from http://www.naacp.org/criminal-justice-fact-sheet/

National Crime Prevention Centre. (2007). *Youth gangs.*

Roesch, R., Zapf, P.A., Golding, S.L., & Skeem, J.L. (1999). Defining and assessing competency to stand trial. *The Handbook of Forensic Psychology, 2*, 327–349.

Sago, R. (2017, August 15). Charging youths as adults can be a 'cruel wake up call.' Is there another way? *National Public Radio.* Retrieved from https://www.npr.org/2017/08/15/542609000/sentenced-to-adulthood-direct-file-laws-bypass-juvenile-justice-system

Sharma, M., Purdy, S.C., & Kelly, A.S. (2009). Comorbidity of auditory processing, language, and reading disorders. *Journal of Speech, Language, and Hearing Research, 52*(3), 706–722.

The Sentencing Project. (2016). *The color of justice: Racial and ethnic disparity in state prisons.* Retrieved from http://www.sentencingproject.org/wp-content/uploads/2016/06/The-Color-of-Justice-Racial-and-Ethnic-Disparity-in-State-Prisons.pdf

Tanielian, T., & Jaycox A.L.H. (2008). *Invisible wounds of war: Psychological and cognitive injuries, their consequences, and services to assist recovery.* Santa Monica, CA: RAND.

Wu J., & Pyrooz, C.D. (2015). Uncovering the pathways between gang membership and violent victimization. *Journal of Quantitative Criminology, 32*(4), 531–558. doi: 10.1007/s10940-015-9266-5

Yurgil, K.A., Barkauskas, D.A., Vasterling, J.J., Nievergelt, C.M., Larson, G.E., Schork, N.J. (2014). Association between traumatic brain injury and risk of posttraumatic stress disorder in active-duty marines. *JAMA Psychiatry, 71*(2), 149–157.

6

WORK PRODUCT (WRITTEN, DEMONSTRATIVE, ORAL)

Hillary Vervalin and Kathleen McGuire

Abstract

This chapter will provide an overview of work product developed by criminal defense-based forensic social workers, how it can be utilized on the legal team and in the courtroom, and limitations to the confidentiality of work product under various circumstances.

Learning Objectives

- Understand confidentiality and legal privilege of work product developed by forensic social workers
- Identify types of work product developed by forensic social workers
- Recognize how each type of work product can be utilized

A criminal defense-based forensic social worker utilizes their skill set and training in social work to produce informative and creative written and demonstrative materials called work product. The purpose of work product is to document the social worker's contact with the client, inform the legal team about the client's life history, provide relevant information to decision-makers involved in the client's case, and validate the client's experience of their past, present, and future. Work product is a tangible, and often visual, way for the forensic social worker to assist in the collaborative efforts of the defense team in achieving the best possible outcome for the client's criminal case.

The creation and utilization of work product to tell a client's story is an area of increasing creativity and aptitude. A forensic social worker creates various types of written and demonstrative materials to powerfully communicate the unique circumstances of client's life including family history and dynamics, risk and protective factors in a developmental context, current functioning, as well as likelihood of rehabilitation in the future. Still, for work product to aid the criminal defense team in effectively telling the client's story, it is imperative that the forensic social worker understands the basic legal principles of work product including confidentiality and privilege.

Confidentiality, Legal Privilege, and Work Product in a Legal Context

The work product doctrine is designed to protect the attorney's mental impressions and legal analysis and allow the attorney the ability to properly analyze the merits of and prepare for the disposition of a client's case (*People v. Martinez*, Colo. 1998), *citing, A. v. District Court*, 550 P.2d 315, 325 (Colo. 1976). Each state or jurisdiction will have their own governing rules or statutes around work product and disclosures. In Colorado, in criminal cases, "work product" is defined as legal research or records, correspondence, reports, and memoranda to the extent that they contain the opinions, theories, or conclusions of the attorney or members of his or her legal staff (Colorado Rules of Criminal Procedure, Rule 16(1)(e)(1)). A defense attorney's work product, as defined earlier, is protected and thus, confidential. The ethical rules requiring confidentiality in the attorney-client relationship, which is the basis for the work product doctrine, extend to individuals employed by or independent contractors of the attorney and require the attorney to be responsible for the work product of individual contractors including criminal defense-based forensic social workers. *See*, ABA Model Rules of Prof'l Conduct R. 1.6 and 5.3. The forensic social worker is an agent of the attorney and, therefore, their work product is protected. This rule, however, is not absolute and disclosure of work product outside the legal team is possible. Communication early and often between the attorney and the forensic social worker on the case regarding possible work product and how it will be utilized including whether it will remain confidential or be disclosed at some point is crucial.

It is imperative that a forensic social worker understands the rules impacting confidentiality and attorney-client privilege, as well as their own ethics as a social worker, as it relates to work product. The criminal defense-based forensic social worker is operating under the rules, guidelines, and statutes governing the practice of lawyers for the state in which they are practicing (See Chapters 2 and 7, "Guiding Principles of Practice" and "Working with Experts," for more information). As described more in depth in Chapter 2, "Guiding Principles of

Practice," there are differences between an attorney and their agents' obligations regarding confidentiality and work product than that of a social worker in a traditional social work role. There are also critical differences between "factual" and "opinion" work product, as well as between providing information as a fact witness and an expert witness, both of which will guide critical decisions on a defense team toward the client's expressed legal interests and will be covered later.

Potential Waiver of Privilege (Disclosure of Otherwise Protected Information)

There are many opportunities in the criminal court process for a defense team to share information about the client, their life history, and their involvement in the crime toward a fair and appropriate resolution of their case. This ordinarily takes the form of mitigation presentations and plea discussions with the prosecution. Additionally, there are times that disclosures will occur because the attorneys raise a particular defense in a criminal case. The nuances of these concepts are beyond the reach of this chapter and book, but an overview of the attorney-client privilege and disclosures or waiver of privilege are developed more thoroughly in Chapter 2, "Guiding Principles of Practice," of this book.

Briefly here, one area of waiver can occur in the form of a social worker's oral advocacy for a client, which will also be discussed as a type of work product later. In a courtroom setting, witnesses typically testify in the capacity of lay, or fact, witness or in the capacity of an expert witness. Fact witnesses testify to their personal knowledge concerning events or some other material or relevant issue in the case. Expert witnesses are permitted to provide an opinion concerning facts, provided that opinion is based on the witness's expertise. In a criminal setting, rules dictate what material must be provided to opposing counsel in any given situation. These rules can vary depending on whether a witness is testifying as a fact witness or an expert witness. Some jurisdictions require both the defense and the prosecution to provide material related to a potential fact witness. Other jurisdictions require only the prosecution to provide material, and the defense has no obligation, in most circumstances, to provide information related to a potential fact witness's testimony. Most jurisdictions, however, have increased disclosure requirements when a witness is testifying as an expert. Under this circumstance, either side would be required to disclose the qualifications of the expert witness, the information that the expert witness relied upon when formulating their opinion, along with the ultimate opinion to which the expert witness would testify (see Chapter 7 "Forensic Social Work and Collaboration with Expert Witnesses" for more information on this topic).

Fact-Witness Testimony

An attorney may ask a social worker to testify as a fact witness for a myriad of purposes, including:

- To summarize information contained within copious records (such as mental health treatment records).
- To provide information concerning statements made by certain witnesses who were interviewed by the forensic social worker.
- To introduce demonstrative aids which would aid the fact-finder (judge or jury) in determining a particular issue.

In preparation for fact-witness testimony, the forensic social worker should closely review the materials that are the basis for the testimony, including records, reports from witness interviews, etc. A fact witness is most credible if they are precise with the information they are providing. For example, if records indicate that neighbors contacted the Department of Human Services on three occasions, the social worker must clearly and accurately report the dates of contact when answering the question as opposed to stating that the neighbor contacted DHS a few times.

When testifying as a fact witness, the social worker likely has clinical opinions about the client but is not allowed to speak about their clinical opinions in this capacity. Let's say the forensic social worker is testifying as a fact witness at a hearing. The attorney wants the social worker to answer questions about their interviews with the client's family, who each reported that the client was sexually abused from ages 2 to 10. The social worker can answer questions regarding who reported the information and what they shared about the client's history of sexual abuse. If discussed during the family interviews, the social worker can answer questions regarding how the sexual abuse negatively impacted the client's life, if a witness talked about this in their interview. However, the social worker cannot state that, based on research, the client experienced significant trauma in childhood which negatively impacted his performance in school, relationships with his family, and increased his proclivity to engage with negative peers, even if that information is clinically accurate. If a fact witness "exceeds [his or her] knowledge in testifying, [the] responses can be struck from the record," thus excluding the testimony from the evidence that the judge or jury can consider when making their decision (Slater & Fink, 2012 p. 174).

As stated previously, what the attorney is required to disclose will vary depending on the state and the rules governing a particular jurisdiction. Even when testifying as a fact witness rather than an expert witness, most jurisdictions require disclosure of the underlying information which forms the basis for the testimony. If the social worker is summarizing copious records, it is likely the defense team will be required to disclose the records along with the social worker's summary report of the records. If the social worker testifies to statements made by a certain witness, those statements, minimally (and perhaps the entire report documenting these statements) will likely be disclosed. Similarly, if the defense team seeks to introduce a demonstrative aid, the underlying documents or reports utilized to prepare the demonstrative aid may likely be disclosed.

It is entirely possible that the basis for a report or demonstrative aid consists of statements made from a client, as opposed to a third-person witness. Whether or not the attorney wishes to disclose these statements is a decision only the attorney can make as they are the person who will be familiar with the rules and obligations governing disclosures and be capable of weighing the benefits and risks of a waiver of attorney-client privilege. Therefore, the forensic social worker should engage in corroborating, to the extent possible, all statements made to avoid compelling the disclosure of statements by a client. This corroboration can occur, for instance, through interviews with third-party witnesses or thorough review of available records of the client's life.

Expert-Witness Testimony

Because disclosures of expert witnesses can be more far-reaching than those of a fact witness, it is important for the forensic social worker to communicate with the attorney early on in the case to determine if he or she could potentially be asked to testify as an expert. It is highly possible, if not probable, that work product will be disclosed if it is relevant to the expert's opinion.

An attorney may ask a social worker to testify as an expert for innumerable reasons. Some of these reasons include:

- To provide testimony concerning specific research or specific aspects of mitigation within the biopsychosocial assessment.
- To provide impressions and opinions concerning the client's level or sincerity of remorse.
- To provide information about the client's reentry potential including their likelihood of rehabilitation and or their functioning or engagement in treatment services.

Because of the intricacies involved in testifying as either a fact or expert witness, some defense teams create systems to insulate or protect the forensic social worker early on in the case to avoid the potential to inadvertently waive privilege or work product. For instance, in Colorado where the defense team is not often required to disclose the work product of its agent investigators, investigative reports become confidential work product. Investigators can have access to the same information as the attorney, including all statements made by a client. Should an investigator testify about a statement made by a particular witness, the report of that witness's prior statement may be required to be disclosed prior to the testimony. The attorney makes decisions about whether to call the investigator as a witness based on this knowledge. A social worker, however, may be privy to far more revealing information that comes directly from the client as opposed to a third party. For instance, a forensic social worker may develop a biopsychosocial assessment based in large part on the statements from the client and may require expert testimony from the social worker to admit the report, depending upon individual circumstances. This may require the forensic social worker to disclose all notes which formed the basis for this assessment, including client interview notes and potentially even notes between the defense team members. Therefore, the defense lawyer may require the social worker to use discretion in all written correspondences with the defense team and may limit the information which the social worker has access to within the defense team as to preserve the sanctity of the attorney-client privilege.

Practical Tips for Testifying

- Communicate early and often with the attorney on the case about the likelihood of testifying and clarify whether the anticipated testimony will be as a fact or opinion witness;
- Understand the basis of the testimony—what information is the attorney trying to elicit from you and for what purpose?;
- Request that the attorney on the case, who will be conducting the direct examination, provides a list of possible questions well in advance;
- Request that the attorney on the case also provides a list of hypothetical questions that the prosecutor may ask on cross-examination;
- Practice answering the sample questions alone;
- Practice both the direct and hypothetical cross-examination with the attorney on the case;
- Be prepared! Review any notes, reports, records, or other relevant information prior to the practice testimony and again before testimony in court.

Case Study #4 (Jamie)

See the following for a reintroduction of Case Study #4: Jamie. Jamie's story will be utilized in all work product examples throughout this chapter.

Jamie is a 14-year-old individual who has no juvenile record and is entering the juvenile court system on charges of trespassing, burglary, and vandalism of her friend Christa's house. Christa is also her codefendant as the two girls allegedly planned to break into Christa's mother's house together. The two girls had not known each other long, and Jamie insists that she did not know that Christa was going to burglarize her own home. Jamie is a freshman in high school and struggling with her identity and lack of familial and social support. Jamie was born as a biological male but has always identified as a female. She recently decided to "come out" to her friends and family, and wants to be referred to using the pronoun "she."

The criminal defense-based social worker meets Jamie at the youth detention center. The social worker is surprised that Jamie is still detained because she has no previous system involvement and is not charged with a crime of violence. Jamie reveals to the social worker that she does not have a good relationship with her parents right now. Jamie states that her parents are divorced, and they are "barely talking to me" because Jamie recently told them that she identifies as a female and would like to be called "she." The social worker concludes that leading up to Jamie's arrest, she was experiencing difficult life changes and has struggled with the lack of support from family and former friends. Jamie also reports that staff at the detention facility are discriminating against her because of her choice to identify as a woman. They are making insensitive comments and continuing to refer to Jamie as "he." Moreover, the facility's policy states that because of her anatomy Jamie must be housed with the adolescent boys which is causing her distress.

The criminal defense-based social worker will be tasked with obtaining Jamie's life history and better assessing what specific stressful life events may have led up to the alleged crime, interviewing family members and friends, and helping to advocate for Jamie at the detention facility. The social worker will also work with Jamie's caseworker through the Department of Human Services. The caseworker opened a Dependency and Neglect case based on Jamie's parents' refusal to bond her out. The forensic social worker will also coordinate with Jamie's guardian ad litem (GAL) to find the most therapeutic place for Jamie to live while her juvenile case progresses through the system. The social worker will also work to find support groups and family therapy options for the family as they work to accept their daughter's identity.

Types of Work Product Generated by a Forensic Social Worker

Written Work Product

The Client Interview Note

See Figure 6.1 for an example of a client interview note with Jamie.

Both social work and legal professionals rely on documentation daily to provide a written record of work on a case including client visits, meetings with other professionals, communication with team members and others in the field, etc. Moreover, social workers across all fields of practice rely heavily on documentation to detail client contact, life-history information, treatment recommendations, etc. While there are many similarities between documentation across social work disciplines, the information included in this chapter regarding documentation and note-taking has been adapted for the defense-based forensic social work role.

One of the most basic forms of work product that a forensic social worker prepares is the "client interview note" which documents contact and interviews with the client throughout the entirety of the case. The term "client interview note" will be used throughout this chapter, as opposed to the more commonly used term in the field of social work, "session note." This distinction is present because forensic social workers are not clinicians or therapists, do not provide therapy, and often meet with clients in non-therapeutic settings like locked detention facilities, jails, or prisons. The authors of this book acknowledge that other terms may be used in various agencies and partnerships across the country.

Documentation of client interviews can take the form of either opinion or factual work product. The most basic form of factual work product a forensic social worker prepares are notes that contemporaneously record the social worker's interviews with their client. This documentation can be statements made by a client or documentation of responses by the client to questions concerning factual matters such as the client's life history. A client interview note can also be a means to document current mental health symptoms, treatment progress, and more. This could be considered opinion, as opposed to factual, work product, particularly when it contains subjective information or opinions from the social worker. Client interview notes must be written in a professional manner, even though they are intended to remain confidential to the defense team, in case they are disclosed during or after the case or after the forensic social worker's involvement on the case has ended.

According to social work literature, there are six main functions of documentation: Assessment and planning, service delivery, continuity and coordination of services, supervision, service evaluation, and accountability to other systems (Kagle, 1995; Luepker & Norton, 2002; Reamer, 2003, 2005). However, for the purposes of a forensic social worker's role on a criminal defense team, this chapter will discuss five of the six roles: Assessment and planning, service delivery, continuity and coordination of services, service evaluation, and accountability to other systems.

1. *Assessment and planning*: Client interview notes help a criminal defense-based social worker document information that the client has shared

about his or her life history, past and current mental health symptoms, experiences of trauma, among other things. It is necessary to document this information to prepare life-history work product, assess and plan for possible interventions, provide treatment recommendations, and advocate for certain case outcomes that prioritize treatment and rehabilitation.

2. *Service Delivery*: Documentation including client interview notes, social worker impressions and opinions, and observations of the client are necessary for delivery of services related to the legal case. When a forensic social worker meets with their client, they might discuss past traumas, goals for the future, processing a death in the family, or challenging faulty cognitions that prohibit a client from emotional growth. The client interview note should document the services the client is receiving from the forensic social worker as well as a summary of the client's interactions with other professionals during that time.
3. *Continuity and Coordination:* Continuity and coordination of services ensure that other professionals such as expert witnesses have access to all the information and insights that the forensic social worker has developed over the course of the case. In essence, continuity of care ensures that other professionals have the same knowledge and information as the social worker while remaining mindful of what information should remain confidential and privileged. Additionally, if the case changes from one social worker to another, detailed client interview notes can help the incoming social worker better understand the client and the case.
4. *Service Evaluation*: Social workers are constantly evaluating their own work including efficacy of interventions with a client or work product development for the legal team. A social worker's documentation of client meetings can help their personal evaluation process. Likewise, the team will also use a social worker's documentation to confirm that the social worker is having the necessary conversations with the client and others. If this information is not documented, it is impossible to evaluate the services provided in any particular case.
5. *Accountability to Other Systems:* Finally, case documentation is necessary for accountability to other systems. Examples include if a social worker testifies in court as an expert, they are required to provide the district attorneys with some or all of the information that they relied upon in reaching a conclusion. If the social worker took poor or inconsistent notes, they are doing a disservice to the client and team. Additionally, if the client filed a grievance against the social worker or legal team, the social worker would likely be required to provide his or her case file including client interview notes for review to either refute or confirm the grievance claims.

Client Interview Note:
Date/time: 1/5/2018: 12:00 PM
Subject: The second interview with Jamie at Cottonwood Juvenile Detention Facility

Presentation:
This social worker met with Jamie today. She presented as tired but engaged. She stated that she was tired because she was "up late and couldn't get to sleep." Jamie appeared healthy and well-nourished and oriented to person, time, and place.

Sleeping and Eating Patterns:
This social worker asked Jamie about her sleeping patterns because she stated that she had trouble falling asleep the night before. Jamie explained that she gets anxiety at night, usually right before bed, and it can prevent her from falling asleep. She stated that her mind "just keeps running and running."

Jamie also stated that she has not been eating "as much as normal" which she explained was typically three meals and two snacks per day. When asked why Jamie's appetite had decreased, she shrugged her shoulders and dropped her head. After a few moments of silence, Jamie went on to say that she is experiencing bullying from the other kids at the detention facility and she avoids eating meals in the dining hall when she can. Jamie lowered her head and began to cry. She stated, "something happened last night" (discussed more thoroughly below).

Peer and Staff Relationships:
Jamie expanded on being bullied by her peers. She stated that she has no friends at the facility and feels very "out of place." Jamie explained that staff is forcing her to stay in the male section of the facility even though she identifies as a woman. She is still forced to shower, change clothing, and sleep in the same pod as the boys. Jamie explained that her peers did not know that she identifies as a woman until one of the staff said something in front of the other residents. Jamie stated, through tears, that she felt betrayed by the staff member and vulnerable and embarrassed that the other kids knew. She clarified that she is not embarrassed about herself and is proud of her choice to come out but did not want anyone at the detention center to know. Jamie continued by explaining that she is very distrusting of others and worried about their disapproval of her identity because of her experience coming out to her parents and friends. Jamie explained that her parents and friends were not approving of her decision to identify openly as a woman and disowned her. Since the staff member told everyone at the facility about two weeks ago, Jamie has experienced bullying every day usually in the dining hall, at shower time, and before bedtime. Jamie also relayed to this social worker an incident that occurred two days ago in which two boys cornered Jamie in the shower area. A staff member disrupted the interaction. Jamie and the staff member discussed what happened, but the staff member only stated that he had not witnessed staff or peers bully Jamie before this conversation. The exchange between Jamie and the staff member ended. Jamie stated that she did not feel any sense of resolution or increased safety. She stated that she felt misunderstood and less important because "I'm different than the other kids."
*A separate memo will detail the 1/4/18 incident in greater detail.

Family Dynamics:
Jamie reported that she has had minimal contact with her parents since our last visit. Her parents are still refusing to bond her out. The social has met with Jamie's parents together one time. They expressed frustration and anger with their daughter for her alleged crime. They denied that they are disappointed with her regarding her identification as a woman.

To Do:

1. Social worker will meet with Jamie's parents separately to begin building rapport and get a better idea of bond options.
2. Social worker will contact attorney and about recent situation at the detention center. Jamie also gave verbal consent to contact parents about the recent situation.
3. Team will work to find a new living situation for Jamie. Explore out-of-custody or treatment facility options with emphasis on support for transgender individuals.

FIGURE 6.1 Client Interview Note

Reports

A report is an objective document that relays specific information from a client, but more often from an interview with a third-party witness. Third-party witnesses consist of a host of individuals, including family members, friends of the client, treatment professionals, or any person other than the client or member of the defense team. It should be noted that the authors of this book utilize the term "report," but acknowledge that other models, partnerships or agencies across the country may use the term "memo" or use the terms "report" and "memo" interchangeably. For purposes of this chapter, the term "report" will be used.

Reports of Third-Party (Mitigation or Life-History Witness) Interviews

Most criminal defense teams include an investigator who is responsible for interviewing witnesses who were present when a crime occurred or know something about the crime or the theory of defense in a case. Forensic social workers also complete interviews but are not involved in the fact-oriented investigation of the underlying criminal charge. Conversely, forensic social workers interview family members or others who can provide information about the client's life history or life leading up to the alleged crime. These third-party witnesses, also called mitigation or life-history witnesses, can include former teachers, mentors, friends, treatment professionals, among others. As explained in Chapter 4, "Skills," it is important for the forensic social worker to meet with and interview mitigation witnesses who can provide information about the client's life history and corroborate events that the client has shared or that are present in client records. Not only does corroborating information reduce the likelihood of disclosure of a client's personal statements, but it also increases the credibility of the information and helps the forensic social worker gain a fuller picture of the client's life. Moreover, there may be instances when the client does not remember an event because he or she was too young. Family members, family friends, or neighbors can help the social worker piece together events in client's life that may be valuable to his or her mitigation narrative. As explained in Chapter 4, "Skills," the forensic social worker is uniquely positioned to obtain life-history information from mitigation witnesses due to training and education in mental health, risk and protective factors, and childhood development. Moreover, the forensic social worker is trained in active listening, rapport building, and trauma-informed care and can likely elicit valuable information from witnesses.

After an interview with a mitigation or third-party witness, the forensic social worker often compiles the information into a factual and objective report for the attorney. Many social workers take notes during an interview to create a report that details the information provided by the witness while ensuring proper and accurate representation of the topics discussed in the interview. The contents of the report may be incorporated into a mitigation report or biopsychosocial assessment to help corroborate the experiences of the client over his or her life.

Generally speaking, a report of an interview of a third-party witness would be considered factual work product because it is simply a recitation of what was said and observed. However, it is possible for a factual work product report to become opinion work product with the insertion of opinions or impressions. For instance, a forensic social worker may interview a family member concerning the client's life history. The report relays not only what was said but the social worker's observations that the witness appeared to be intoxicated or "in denial" of some fact or any one of many thoughts and opinions about a witness. This inclusion changes the report from solely factual information to opinion as well.

Reports of Events, Incidents, or Circumstances

See Figure 6.2 for an example of a report written after Jamie was threatened at the youth detention center.

In addition to writing reports following third-party or mitigation witness interviews, a forensic social worker can write a report relaying objective information about an event that took place with a client or other witness. Let's delve deeper into Jamie's case and how the forensic social worker should document an event that took place at the detention facility.

The criminal defense-based social worker meets Jamie at the youth detention center for their second meeting and records the information in the client interview note (Figure 6.1).

Jamie tells the social worker about an incident that occurred at the facility the night before with two male residents which is documented in Figure 6.2. Jamie is concerned for her safety, believes she is being discriminated against, and wants to leave the facility immediately.

The social worker makes a note to contact the attorney on Jamie's case right after the visit, as well Jamie's Department of Human Services caseworker and GAL to discuss alternative, therapeutic placement options for Jamie. Based on the Prison Rape Elimination Act that became federal law in 2003, Jamie is required certain safety considerations, including showering separately from other residents as a person who identifies as transgender. So far, the PREA laws have not been enacted at Cottonwood Detention Facility based on Jamie's report to her forensic social worker. Moreover, the lack of PREA enforcement created an environment where the incident with Jamie and the other boys could occur (Prison Rape Elimination Act of 2003, 115.342). The forensic social worker on Jamie's case will recommend that the attorney contact a juvenile civil rights attorney to consult with the team and help advocate for a more appropriate placement for Jamie immediately. The team will also need to work with Jamie's family at length to understand their beliefs and biases which have impacted their ability to accept their daughter and support her throughout this process of transition. (Please visit the reference section of this chapter for a citation of the PREA: Juvenile Facility Standards.)

Memo:
Date: 1/6/2018
Subject: 1/4/2018 incident at Cottonwood Detention Center
Client: Jamie Andrews, 18JD13

This social worker met with Jamie on 1/5/2016 at Cottonwood Detention Facility. She reported an incident that occurred at the facility with another resident at 9:45 PM on 1/4/2018. She stated that she is being housed in the male pod at the detention facility because she is biologically a male. The detention staff has not made any accommodations for Jamie based on her choice to identify as a female.

On 1/4/2018, Jamie took her nightly shower. In the shower area, two of the male residents cornered her. She stated that she was very fearful and concerned for her well-being. As the two boys moved closer to Jamie, they called her derogatory names in a threatening tone. Fortunately for Jamie, a male staff member, Jason, entered the shower and asked Jamie and the two boys what they were doing. The boys responded that they were finishing their showers and left the area. Jamie stated that she was upset and crying as the boys left. Jason told Jamie to get ready for bed and that they would discuss what happened in Jason's office in thirty minutes. Jamie told Jason what happened but also stated that she was fearful for her safety moving forward. Jamie explained that she has been exposed to bullying and discrimination since it was revealed that she identifies as a female. She continued by stating that this recent experience has made her even more fearful for her physical safety. Jason stated that he has not witnessed any staff or residents bullying Jamie and that he "does not see what the big deal is anyway about a little bullying. It happens all the time around here." The interaction between Jamie and Jason ended.

When this social worker visited Jamie on 1/5/18, she had not had any other conversations with staff members about the incident. There have not been any accommodations made for Jamie or planning around how to increase her safety and improve her comfort level.

End report.

FIGURE 6.2 Report

To summarize, client interview notes and reports can take the form of both fact and opinion work product and may contain sensitive, confidential, and subjective information about a myriad of subjects including a client's history of trauma or the facts of the case. Both client interview notes and reports of third-party interviews should be prepared in a professional manner with the understanding that these notes or reports may be turned over to others outside the defense team. The decision whether to disclose client interview notes or reports remains with the attorney and, ultimately, the client, keeping in mind their expressed legal interests.

Complex, Written Work Product

Complex forms of work product include written documents that detail the client's full life history like a biopsychosocial assessment or feature an important piece of the mitigation narrative like a mitigation report.

Biopsychosocial Assessments

See Figure 6.3 for an excerpt of a forensic social worker's biopsychosocial assessment for Jamie.

A biopsychosocial assessment is a thorough examination and review of a client's life history, considering biological, psychological, sociological, and spiritual risk and protective factors, in a developmental context, that have contributed to a client's hardships or successes in life. See Chapter 4, "Skills," for a detailed explanation of risk and protective factors and the developmental assessment. As briefly defined in Chapter 4, "Skills," the biopsychosocial model of analyzing and understanding a person was created and used for more thorough medical care by George Engel in 1977. He believed that the medical community was focused on a limited view of patients as objects which ignored the individual and subjective experience of each person (Borrell-Carrio, Suchman, & Epstein, 2004; Engel, 1977). The social work profession has utilized the biopsychosocial assessment to obtain a full picture of the client prior to providing a diagnosis or treatment recommendations. The legal field has begun to do the same. Just as a doctor and treating psychiatrists needs to understand the many facets that make up a patient, so should the legal community to provide the most comprehensive intervention and treatment recommendations available.

A biopsychosocial assessment, which may have a different title in other forensic social work settings, is a comprehensive document that is most often utilized to inform the legal team and expert witnesses about the client's life history. (See Chapter 7, "Forensic Social Work and Collaboration with Expert Witnesses," to better understand the utilization of a biopsychosocial assessment to inform an expert.) A full biopsychosocial assessment should be an exhaustive examination of a client's life utilizing information from the client, mitigation interviews, records, and historical data if relevant. The forensic social worker should refrain from providing clinical opinions about the client and their life history as this is the expert's role. Moreover, a factual biopsychosocial assessment should allow for the forensic social worker to testify as a fact witness about the client's life without any concern that the document provides an expert analysis that is beyond the reach of the social worker as a fact witness.

Complex Work Product—Mitigation Reports

See Figure 6.4 for an excerpt of a forensic social worker's mitigation report for Jamie.

A mitigation report is similar to a biopsychosocial assessment but narrows the scope of the report to focus solely on information that is relevant to the facts of the case or mitigation surrounding the case. While the biopsychosocial assessment discusses several important life events and outlines numerous risk and protective factors that may have impacted the client, a mitigation report will only focus on thematic risk and protective factors that may have contributed

Forensic Biopsychosocial Assessment | Social Worker's Name
Client: Andrews, Jamie; 18CR13 | Title

III. Early Childhood Development and Family Dynamics: Age 0-5 (2003-2008)

a. Prenatal Factors, Birth, and First Milestones

On October 10th, 2003, Jamie was born in Lamar, Colorado. Both William and Patricia reported that Patricia had a healthy pregnancy and delivery with Jamie. Jamie was delivered full-term and reportedly met all developmental milestones on time. According to William, Jamie was walking at 11 months old and saying small phrases and sentences by 18 months, although he did not remember the exact age. From age zero to five, both William and Patricia described Jamie as a happy, outgoing, and fun-loving child.

b. William and Patricia's Divorce

In March of 2006, when Jamie was about 3-years-old, the Andrews family moved from Lamar, Colorado to Denver, Colorado. Patricia was laid off from her job as a paralegal at a struggling law firm, and William owned a small real estate business that did not make ends meet for the family in Lamar. Patricia found a job in Denver, and the family moved. Within nine months of moving to Denver, William's real estate business grew exponentially, and he hired a secretary and two other agents to work with him. At the same time, Patricia's was promoted at the large family law firm where she worked. Both William and Patricia expressed that they were disconnected from each other and dissatisfied with their marriage. Patricia felt like William was unsupportive and closed off. William stated that Patricia was more concerned with her promotion than supporting and celebrating William's business growth. William and Patricia both refused to admit who had an affair first, but after one and a half years in Denver, both parties had been unfaithful to each other. William even had a girlfriend. He filed for divorce, and the family home became a hostile environment.

When asked whether there was noticeable fighting or tension in the home prior to or during the divorce, William stated that Jamie "screamed and cried every time Patricia and I yelled at each other. It was heartbreaking but difficult to stop- almost like a train wreck" (Personal Communication, February 31st, 2018). Jamie did not recall any of the fights in the home because she was only 3-4 years old, but she stated that their tumultuous relationship and inabilities to co-parent have "definitely hurt me over the years" (Personal Communication, February 5th, 2018). Jamie's older siblings, Jennifer (26 now, but 13 at the time) and Richard (20 now, but 7 at the time), were both involved in sports, other extracurricular activities, and spent time with friends. Richard was home more than his teenage sister and recalled "constant" (Personal Communication, February 25th, 2018). Even at the young age of 7, Richard often went to a friend's house to escape the hostile environment but noted that Jamie was only 3-years-old and was forced to endure the chaotic and tenuous home environment all of the time.

William and Patricia finalized their divorce in July of 2008 when Jamie was 5-years-old. The next several years of Jamie's life included a heart wrenching and traumatic custody battle between her parents and their new spouses and children. There were fights about property, vacation time, parenting abilities and rights, child support payments, and even who loved and wanted Jamie more. The divorce records indicated that Patricia stated in court, "William never wanted children, and he does not love Jamie as much as I do" (p.141 of divorce records). William's attorney referred to Patricia as "petty, materialistic, and vindictive" (p.159 of divorce records).

FIGURE 6.3 BPS (Biopsychosocial) Report

to the client's alleged offense or the circumstances that allowed for the offense to occur. A mitigation report may also suggest treatment and/or resources for the client that relate back to the risk factors or criminogenic needs of the client to stop the cycle of criminality and decrease the likelihood recidivism, as

Mitigation Report
Client: Andrews, Jamie; 18CR13

Social Worker's Name
Title

V. Adolescent Development: Age 12-present (2016-2018)

a. Jamie Comes Out to Her Family

Prior to Jamie's choice to "come out" to her family and friends, she did well in school, was involved in academic and extracurricular activities, talked to her parents frequently, and learned to manage the once-difficult relationship with and between her parents after their divorce. However, once Jamie began to struggle with her internal sense of self and identity, she became withdrawn. Jamie did not tell her parents about her gender identity. Rather, Jamie's mother read her journal and told Jamie's father. Not only did Jamie feel devastated by the lack of support from her family, but she also felt betrayed that her mother looked at her private journal. The realization that her mother invaded her personal space and betrayed her trust, by not only reading her journal but telling Jamie's father, caused Jamie to isolate even further and begin to associate with negative peers.

b. Jamie Loses Familial and Social Support

After Jamie confirmed to her family that she identifies as a woman and would like to begin transitioning, her parents made their disapproval clear by kicking her out of both of their homes. Jamie stayed with a close friend of many years named Justina. However, when Jamie told Justina what had happened, Justina excluded Jamie for their long-time friend group and even limited how long Jamie could stay with her. Justina also swore she would not tell any of their friends. Unfortunately, after Jamie told Justina what happened, she felt that their friends also started treating her differently and suspected Justina told them.

c. Jamie Finds a New Peer Group out of Desperation and Loneliness

With a lack of familial and social support, Jamie asked her brand-new friend Christa, who she had known for about a week, if she could stay with her. Over the next few days, Christa did cocaine every day. Jamie had just begun to experiment with marijuana, cocaine, and opioid pills at Christa's introduction to numb the emotional pain of her family's rejection and disapproval. Moreover, Christa had an older boyfriend who was a drug dealer and had access to drugs all the time. Christa's father was a business owner and never home. Jamie recalled that she did not see Christa's father once during that time. Sadly, Jamie did not talk to her family during this time either. They ignored her calls and did not respond to her text messages. They even failed to respond her text stating that she was alive after being kicked out of the home.

It is evident based on the timeline of events that Jamie became involved with a delinquent peer group only because she had lost the support and acceptance of her family. Research indicates that one of the strongest predictors of behavior during teenage years is peer association, especially regarding substance use and violent behavior (Hawkins, Catalano & Miller, 1992). Prinstein, Boergers, and Spirito (2001) found that family dysfunction, social acceptance, and depression increased a teenager's likelihood to associate with peers who engage in high-risk behavior. Moreover, the researchers found that high levels of family dysfunction, specifically, were associated with negative peer associations and high-risk behaviors including weapon carrying, cigarette use, marijuana use, and suicidal behavior.

FIGURE 6.4 Mitigation Report

well as improve the person's chances for success in the future. For example, a mitigation report may be helpful for an adult client who is facing his fourth conviction for driving under the influence (DUI). If the client has been an alcoholic for many years, the mitigation report will likely focus exclusively on risk factors that increased their likelihood of becoming an alcoholic including trauma and family genetics. The report may also detail past treatment attempts, cite information from treatment records that appear to have inhibited treatment or made past attempts unsuccessful, and suggest possible treatment options for the client in the community based on their unique history. A mitigation report will use research thoughtfully and sparingly to bolster points about the specific and relevant risk and protective factors. Social sciences research can also be used to support the recommendation of a specific evidence-based treatment. On the other hand, a biopsychosocial assessment is often used for an expert and does not incorporate research, as the purpose is to help inform an expert who will then assert opinions and provide research in their work product. It is important to note that the authors of this book acknowledge that different forensic social workers, agencies, and partnerships may use different terminology or formats for biopsychosocial and mitigation reports.

When writing a mitigation report, it is important for the forensic social worker to know who will be receiving this report and whom the attorney wishes to potentially educate by sharing the report. For example, if the attorney asks the forensic social worker to prepare a mitigation report for use at a sentencing hearing, it is important for the social worker to have information about the judge including what he or she finds important or persuasive. For instance, one judge may not find that childhood abuse is a particularly compelling piece of the mitigation narrative but may be persuaded by issues related to the high cost of incarceration. This could result in a mitigation report which focuses on research related to the link between childhood abuse and potential future incarceration, and the benefits of community-based treatment to address the issues related to past trauma and ultimately reduce recidivism. Likewise, if the social worker writes a mitigation report to help with plea negotiations, it is also important that he or she has information about the district attorney(s) assigned to the case including what kind of mitigation information they values, what information they do not find compelling, whether they are persuaded by relevant social science research, among other pertinent personal and professional attributes of the intended audience.

Complex Work Product—Demonstrative Aids

A demonstrative aid is a visual form of work product to help explain important aspects of a client's life history. The most common examples of demonstrative aids prepared by forensic social workers include but are not limited to time lines, genograms, and ecomaps. Demonstrative aids are a variation of the information presented in written work product and aid in the visual presentation of a client's life history. Demonstrative aids can provide clarity to the audience through illustration of meaningful information, particularly patterns or important overarching themes about the client's life history, current functioning, and reentry potential. Additionally, the process of creating demonstratives aids can be done with the help of a client. While this is not required and may not be appropriate for every client depending upon the level of cognitive functioning, memory, and the rapport and engagement built with the social worker, etc., many individuals are visual learners and can benefit from understanding their own family or life history better. The process of analyzing and understanding one's life history can be empowering and an important way for the client to engage with the team and assist in their own defense.

Genograms

See Figure 6.5 for a genogram of Jamie's family.

The genogram is a visual tool to display family relationships, medical history, personality traits, and much more. The genogram was intended to be a quick reference for family therapists and practitioners to visualize and better understand familial patterns and dynamics that subsist across generations (Hartman & Laird, 1983; McGoldrick & Gerson, 1985). The criminal defense-based forensic social worker utilizes a genogram in a similar way. The purpose is to provide a visual representation of a client and his or her immediate family, including important life events, illnesses, addictions, and other familial issues or relationships between members of the family. The visual nature of the genogram helps to easily detect familial patterns and dynamics over multiple generations that may not be recognizable through note-taking alone. While including the immediate family in the genogram is most beneficial, social workers try to include three generations of family (if the information is available) to get the best representation of transgenerational patterns like addiction and trauma.

The genogram can help the forensic social worker and the legal team visualize and record data regarding a large family or family with many dynamics, such as abuse, divorce, substance abuse, gang membership, and other issues which may have impacted the client during developmental years. This visual data can also help contextualize a client's current or past behaviors by illustrating a pattern of behavior. Patterns of behavior across generations can be mitigating for the client's case including a familial history of mental illness or addiction, which necessitates treatment as opposed to punishment. Let's take a look at Jamie's family history and a basic genogram that the forensic social worker creates to remember the family member's names, ages, and characteristics.

The social worker prepares a family genogram with Jamie to better assess historical and current family dynamics and patterns. Jamie has one older sister, Jennifer, and one older brother, Richard. Jamie has a very good relationship with her siblings despite her current, distant relationship with her parents. Unfortunately, both of Jamie's siblings live out of state and cannot provide additional support at the moment. Jamie's mother, Patricia, and father, William, were married in 1990 and divorced 13 years ago in 2005. Patricia remarried about 4 years after the divorce and had two more children. William remarried very shortly after his divorce from Patricia was final. The family suspects that he was involved in an extra-marital affair with the woman that is now his wife. They do

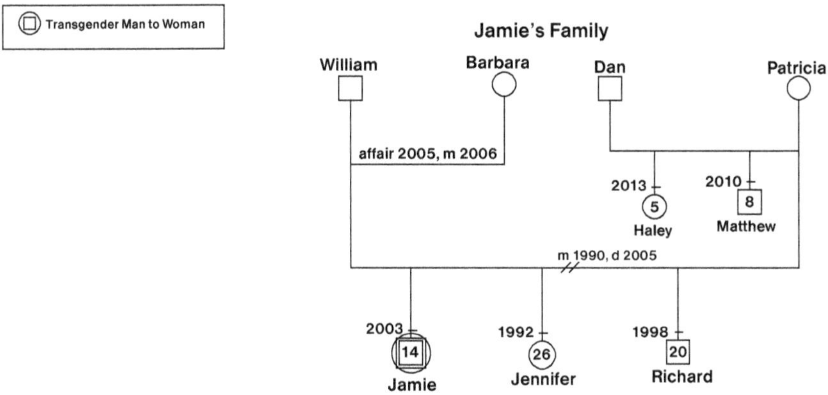

FIGURE 6.5 Genogram

not have children. The family reports no history of addiction or mental illness. Jennifer, who was born in 1992 and is now 26 years old, is a veterinary technician in New Jersey and functioning well. Richard, who was born in 1998 and is now 20 years old, is in his junior year at a university out of state and is currently studying abroad in Amsterdam. The social worker notes that both of Jamie's siblings experienced delinquency as teenagers but appear to be functioning well today. The social worker explores this with the family and finds that William has always worked between 60 and 80 hours a week, often traveling for work, while Patricia has been consumed by her new family and raising her small children. It seems that both Jennifer and Richard were impacted by Patricia and William's divorce and busy lives as well, which became evident in adolescence for both teenagers. Both Jennifer and Richard stated that they felt forgotten and unwanted, so they chose to rebel. Fortunately, once they rebelled, William and Patricia recognized that they needed more guidance and care. It seems that family support helped guide both siblings away from delinquent behavior and back to pro-social behavior. The social worker on Jamie's case needs to be aware that Jamie's conflict with her parents, and her parents' disapproval of her choice to identify as a woman, create additional dynamics and difficulties that Jennifer and Richard did not experience. The additional family dynamics may hinder or delay Jamie's path back to pro-social behavior due to added risk factors although through no fault of her own.

Time Lines

See Figure 6.6 for a time line of Jamie's life leading up to the crime.

A time line is a visual aid that depicts life events in chronological order. A time line can also help to show cause and effect. For instance, sometimes an event, like a criminal charge, takes place because there was an important and often negative life event preceding it. A time line can be a powerful means of demonstrating the impact of risk factors on behaviors and events that follow, or,

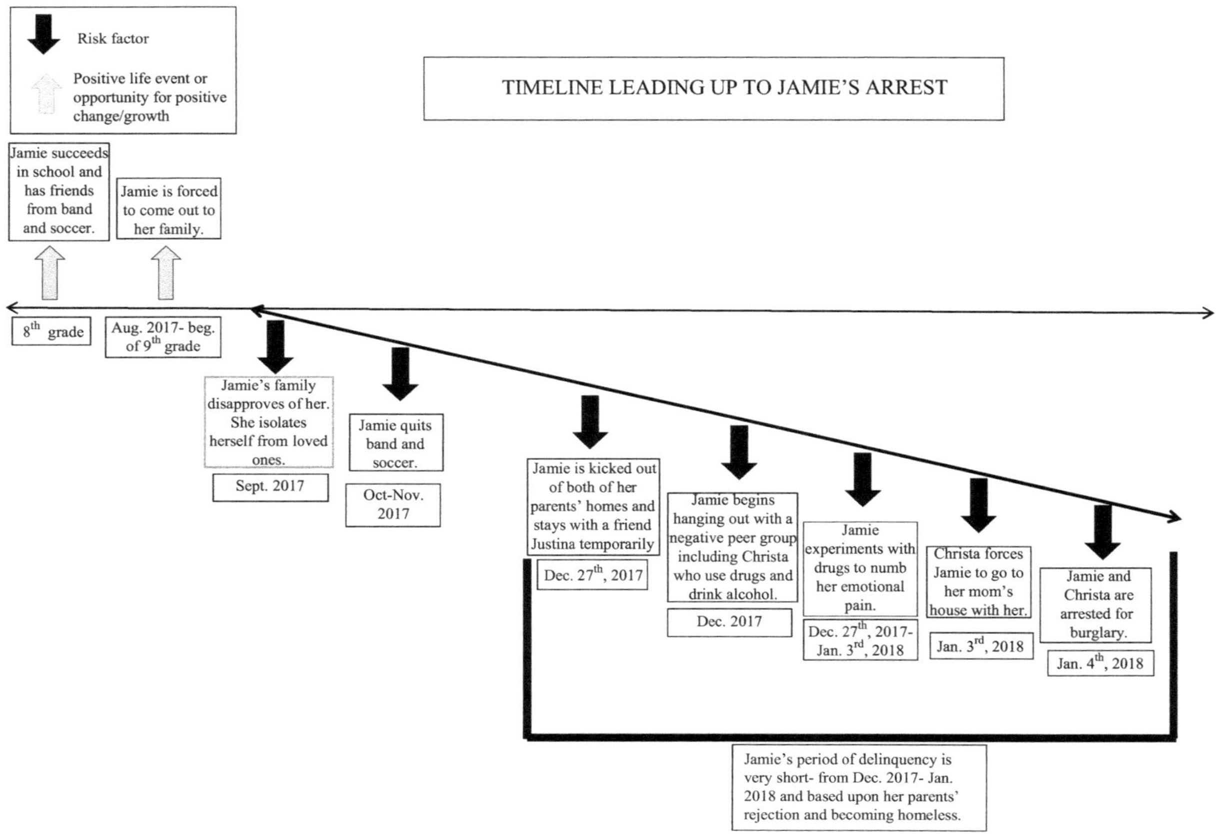

FIGURE 6.6 Time Line

conversely, the absence of maladaptive events and behavior when protective factors are present. A time line can also show the impact of the crime itself on the client's behavior and feelings of remorse in those circumstances where a client takes positive steps to address fluid risk factors following his or her incarceration.

In looking at Jamie's case again, she was always a good student and involved in extracurricular activities including soccer and band. She had a small but tight-knit group of friends. These protective factors allowed Jamie to withstand her father's hectic work schedule and cope with feeling forgotten by her mother and her new family. However, it appeared that when Jamie finally decided that she was ready to openly identify as a woman at the beginning of ninth grade, she lost a great deal of support from her network of mostly religious and conservative individuals, who did not agree with her choice to identify as a woman. During her ninth-grade year, Jamie stopped spending time with her small group of friends, began to fight with her parents often, and quit activities that she had always enjoyed. These events all precipitated Jamie's choice to experiment with drugs and alcohol and associate with a new, negative friend group including Christa, who becomes her codefendant in a matter of days.

Ecomaps

See Figure 6.7 for an example of Jamie's ecomap prior to the crime.

The ecomap was created in the 1970s by Dr. Ann Hartman and was adapted from general systems and person-in-environment theories to visually display the ecosystems that make up human communities (Hartman, 1979). The purpose of an ecomap is to illustrate how a client interacts with his or her environment in positive or negative ways by demonstrating the respective positive or negative influences in a person's life, including people, activities, institutions, etc. For instance, a forensic social worker can create an ecomap that represents the client's life leading up to an alleged criminal act and includes the negative influences like negative friends, drugs, etc. that were present for the person. On the other hand, an ecomap can demonstrate the positive changes the same client has made since his commission of criminal behavior including enrolling in school, finding work, meeting new friends, attending AA or NA, etc. A set of ecomaps that depict before and after visuals of a client's life can be a powerful visual tool for a team, expert, a judge, or, in certain circumstances, even a jury. An ecomap can also help to show how many different systems are involved in a client's life like a GAL, DHS, pre-trial release, drug and alcohol treatment, etc. Moreover, the ecomap can include relationship indicators which are used to show the degree of stress or strength that a relationship or institution has in a person's life. An ecomap can also incorporate relationship indicators such as stressful, tenuous, or positive and the thickness of the line can represent the intensity of the said relationship indicator. Also, an arrow can show which way the energy of the relationship flows and whether this is increasing stress or adding strength and stability for the individual.

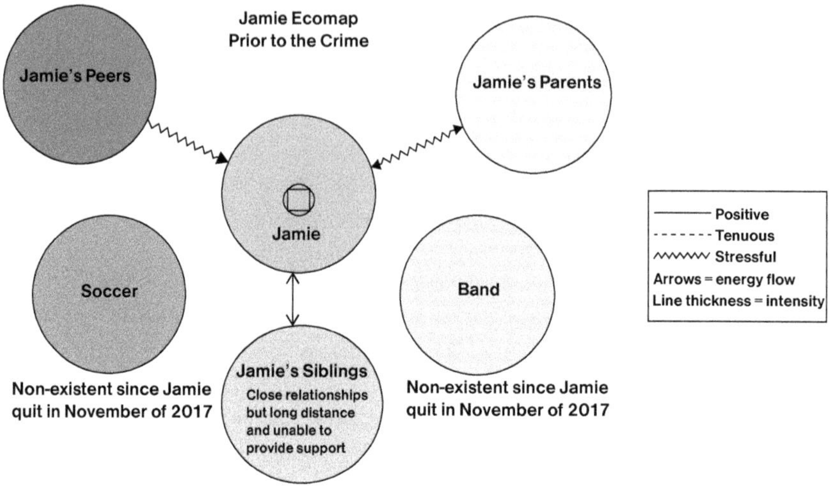

FIGURE 6.7 Ecomap

Let's look at how the ecomap might help illustrate Jamie's life leading up to her arrest. As the social worker begins to delve into Jamie's life, she notices that Jamie had several networks that used to provide her with support and positive outlets including family, friends, band, and soccer. Leading up to her arrest, she had a very stressful relationship with her peer group and parents because of her choice to come out and had no positive outlets because she quit band and soccer. She still had the support of her older siblings, but they are adults now and live elsewhere in the country.

Variations of Ecomaps

See Figure 6.8 for a variation of Jamie's ecomap to include her friend relationships and dynamics the year before the crime and Figure 6.9 for the year leading up to the crime.

As stated earlier, an ecomap can represent the positive or negative influences in a person's life. Social workers on defense teams have found creative ways to show the kinds of influences, also referred to throughout this book as risk and protective factors, that may have impacted a person leading up to a crime. Moreover, a present or future ecomap can illustrate how protective factors or resources that a person engages with including drug treatment, individual and/or family therapy, etc. can improve the stress levels in one's life and lead to more positive actions and behaviors.

An extremely helpful tool that this author created when working with a juvenile client, who had a particularly complicated friend group that was impacting her ability to make better choices and stay away from criminal activity, was a friend map. Because juveniles and young adults are often influenced by peer associations, the friend map can help illustrate for others just how stressful or limiting certain friendships can be and how the absence of those or similar relationships in the future can positively impact a young person's life. As with a basic ecomap, the friend map contains relationship indicators that illustrate the kind of relationship the client has with a friend or even the entire friend group, and the thickness of the line represents the intensity of the said relationship indicator while the arrows show which way the energy of the relationship flows.

Let's continue to discuss Jamie as an example. So far, Jamie has only discussed her new friend and codefendant, Christa. Jamie has a difficult time talking about her old friend group because the deterioration of those relationships over the past year is painful for her. Jamie was best friends with her previous friend group from 1st to 8th grade. They all went to elementary and middle school together and participated in band and soccer both in and out of school. The fact that her best friends turned their back on Jamie when she needed them the most, and after Jamie divulged something very personal and sensitive, has caused her a great deal of pain. After the forensic social worker has built trust with Jamie, Jamie finally begins to open up about some of her old and newer friends. The forensic social worker begins to see that Jamie had very stressful peer relationships leading up to her arrest. Jamie's old friends include Justina, Mary, Jessica, and Jordan. Jamie's old friends, which will be referred to as the "good kids" as Jamie called them, were a group that Jamie identified with in the past. However, she does not relate to them now because her life has changed. Moreover, she has lost trust and confidence in them. They have not supported her choice to come out as a woman. Jamie knows in her heart that she deserves friends who will support her choices no matter what.

For Jamie's legal case, Figure 6.8 shows that Jamie had strong relationships with her friends, who were all engaged in positive behaviors. As a result of the support and positive peer influences, Jamie's behavior was positive as well. Although this tends to simplify the complex dynamics that make up a person's life and relationships, it can depict the power of peers influences in a teenager's life.

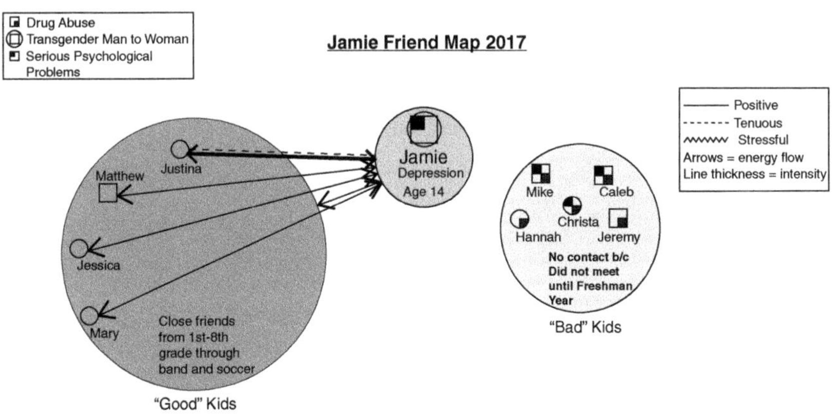

FIGURE 6.8 Friend (Good) Map

On the other hand, Jamie's new friends seemed to be taking advantage of Jamie's kindness and desperation for accepting friends but not providing her with much in return. This dynamic was also very stressful and unfulfilling for Jamie. When Christa and Jamie met, Christa was in a relationship with an older teenage boy named Mike. Mike was friends with Caleb and Brian, who were two 19-year-old drug dealers. Mike had a group of male friends who supplied Christa and Jamie with drugs and alcohol. Unbeknownst to Jamie, Christa had been struggling with suicidal ideations and drug addiction for 2 years prior to meeting Jamie. Christa's mental health symptoms and addiction to drugs worsened when she met Mike. Jamie shared with her social worker through teary eyes that she had saved up money from her allowance. She hoped to leave town and escape her disapproving and unaccepting family and start over. Instead, Jamie's new "friends" forced her to buy drugs from Brian and Caleb for the group when Christa, Mike's girlfriend, reached her limit of free drugs. They threatened to beat up Jamie if she did not comply with their demands. The forensic social worker learned that not only did Jamie spend all her money on drugs for her new "friends," but she felt unsafe and threatened by them on a consistent basis. The forensic social worker's goal in creating the second friend map was to show the stressful and unhealthy relationships that existed in Jamie's life prior to her alleged participation in the burglary. The two friend maps, comparing Jamie's social circle in 2017 and 2018, coupled with the time line in Figure 6.9 effectively demonstrate that Jamie was on a downward spiral toward personal destruction. The two friend maps also show that Jamie had much more stable friendships in 2017 and thus, less stress in her life and no drug use or delinquent behavior. The stress of her friendships coupled with her family's rejection and her struggle with her own identity in 2018 led Jamie to make poor friend and life choices and trust in the wrong individuals which, in part, led to her arrest. These visuals would go very well in the mitigation report to help highlight the complex and contrasting friend groups and experiences in those groups between 2017 and 2018, which undoubtedly impacted her mental health, and critical thinking and decision-making abilities.

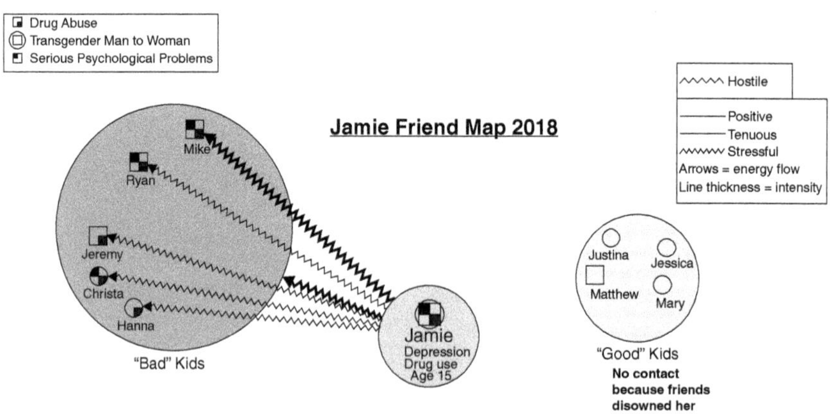

FIGURE 6.9 Friend (Bad) Map

Reentry and Sentencing Reports

As explained previously in this chapter, the vast majority of criminal cases are resolved through a process commonly referred to as "plea bargaining." This generally means that a person agrees to enter a guilty plea to receive a reduction in charges or a reduced, or more favorable, sentence. Written work product can be a useful means of documenting reentry potential and providing recommendations for sentencing. Reentry and sentencing reports are documents prepared by forensic social workers that help explain to a district attorney or judge what the circumstances of a client's life would and could be if he or she lived in the community and received community-based resources and support. Such reports are often categorized by criminogenic needs (see Chapter 4, "Skills"), including future risk and protective factors and access to treatment and rehabilitative options in the community to meet those needs.

Reentry Reports

A reentry report generally focuses on a client who has been in a locked facility such as a jail, prison, or a mental health institute and has the opportunity for release into the community. This report would focus on the client prior to his or her commission of the crime that led to incarceration and treatment the client has engaged in while in custody including the client's independent efforts to grow and change. Ideally, the information regarding the client's period of incarceration would be supported by the records from the facility or facilities where the individual was resided. Moreover, the reentry report would focus on community resources to address ongoing risk factors including mental health, substance abuse and relapse potential, housing and job resources, and community and family support.

Sentencing Reports

See Figure 6.10 for an example of an excerpt of a sentencing report used in Jamie's case.

A forensic social worker generally creates a sentencing report for the client's sentencing hearing after he or she pleads guilty and is awaiting the type and length of punishment that the judge will impose. The general kind of punishment (i.e., probation, jail time, a prison sentence, etc.) is usually known ahead of time because pleading guilty to certain crimes may require by law the completion of a specific sentence which will vary from state to state and at the federal level. Other sentencing agreements may allow for the defendant to have an opening sentencing range in which the judge has full discretion to sentence the individual to anything from probation to jail or prison. In an instance where an open sentence has been achieved, a sentencing or mitigation report can be

Mitigation Report
Client: Andrews, Jamie; 18CR13

Social Worker's Name
Title

II. Cottonwood Detention Facility

Jamie was detained at Cottonwood Detention Facility for 22 days at which point her father bonded her out and agreed to intensive, in-home family therapy. Jamie has no juvenile record and never received treatment prior to her arrest. According to records from Cottonwood Detention Facility, Jamie received no disciplinary write-ups over the 22 days despite experiencing bullying, discrimination, and unsafe situations due to her choice to identify as a female (p.32 of Cottonwood Detention Facility records). On January 4th, 2018, shortly after Jamie was first detained, Jamie was cornered and threatened by two males in her pod while taking her nightly shower. Jamie's legal team was able to advocate for her safety and get her moved into an intake pod where new kids are coming and going daily from the facility. Jamie had more anonymity in the intake pod and felt safer until she was able to return home. Despite feeling unsafe, physically and emotionally while at Cottonwood, Jamie did not break any rules or cause disturbances. Moreover, her teachers noted that she participated in school and received all A's (p.54 of Cottonwood Detention Facility records). Her grades in detention are comparable to her grades from elementary to middle school before she experienced challenging life events including the painful aftermath of coming out as transgender to her family and friends.

III. Treatment and Sentencing Considerations

In reviewing Jamie's life history and the events leading up to the crime, she was homeless, lacking support from the people in her life, experimenting with drugs and alcohol, and struggling to get through every day. It is evident that the antecedent to her delinquent behavior was an immense change in her life- coming out as transgender. It is also evident that Jamie needed to address the disrupted and suffering relationships in her life and find positive supports to help her as she continued to transition.

Jamie has been in the community and receiving intensive, in-home family therapy with her father. Jamie's mother also attends bi-monthly family therapy sessions. Jamie, Jamie's parents, and the family therapist all report that the family's communication has improved greatly. Once Jamie's parents had more insight into Jamie's lack of support from her old friend group, the negative influences of Jamie's temporary peer group, and how their response to their daughter impacted her decision-making process, they apologized and seemed to understand how they could have sought help to handle the situation more appropriately.

In addition to improving the relationship with her parents through family therapy, Jamie's legal team connected her with a mentor who is also transgender. The mentor has helped Jamie navigate her new life and continue the process of transitioning. The mentor has been invaluable to Jamie and helped her see that she is capable of rebuilding the relationships in her life and fostering new ones as she continues to form her identity.

While on bond, Jamie demonstrated an openness to treatment and impressive insight into her behaviors. She has worked with a family therapist, an individual therapist, and continued to work with this social worker. Jamie now understands the importance of choosing a pro-social group of friends and conversely, how quickly a negative friend group can bring a person down. Jamie has demonstrated an amenability to continued treatment in the community and would not benefit from serving any more time in a juvenile facility. Not only does Jamie have specific treatment needs and safety considerations based on her first experience at Cottonwood Detention Facility, but Jamie has already begun the process of rehabilitation in the community and deserves the opportunity to continue.

FIGURE 6.10 Sentencing

extremely helpful in advocating for the lower range of the sentence and the least-restrictive setting where the sentence can be served (i.e., probation in the community, community corrections at a halfway house or drug rehabilitation center, or jail instead of prison) which will allow for the greatest degree of rehabilitation based on access resources and services, education, family support, etc.

The social worker prepares the sentencing report for a judge's consideration. The sentencing report takes into account the client's life history prior to the commission of the crime including risk factors that may have increased the likelihood for unlawful behavior and work the client has done in custody or in the community to turn his life around. The report also argues for a specific sentence that is in line with sentencing guidelines but is the least-restrictive and most rehabilitative. For example, a sentencing report should not argue for probation if the client is not probation eligible. A sentencing report will also focus on criminogenic needs and argue for rehabilitation for the client in a setting that is realistic and in line with the client's identified needs.

Oral Work Product

Advocacy on the Defense Team

As explained in Chapters 4 and 6, "Skills" and "Work Product," of this book, social workers are in a unique position on the criminal defense team to get to know their client very well and build rapport and trust in a slow and methodical way. This relationship between the forensic social worker and the client allows the client to tell the social worker very personal and sensitive information, not only about their past but also about what is happening with the client presently. Social workers are advocates in nearly every field of practice, but it can be very useful on an interdisciplinary team in which other team members have different training, education, work experience, and personalities. A forensic social worker should always be thinking about the client and his or her best interest, whereas a lawyer or investigator may be thinking about the client's best interest from a legal perspective. While both are extremely important to consider, they may not always align. It is imperative that the social worker be the voice for the client and their personal needs, even if the client's legal needs take precedence in the end.

Plea Negotiations and Mitigation Presentations

As stated earlier, many cases are resolved during the plea negotiation phase in which a client agrees to plead guilty to a lesser charge and receive a lesser punishment. Many plea negotiations, especially on high-profile and/or serious cases, are agreed upon after a mitigation presentation in which the defense team prepares pertinent information about the client's life history, mental health, cognitive functioning, etc. The goals of a mitigation presentation include helping the district attorney(s) who are prosecuting the client's case better understand the client's mitigation narrative and ultimately agree to a reduced conviction and punishment. Because the forensic social worker knows the client extremely well and has gathered all the information related to their life history, including client and mitigation interviews, record collecting and reviewing, and assessment writing, the forensic social worker should be present at the meeting and an active participant that is again, advocating for the client.

Oral Advocacy at Sentencing Hearings

Beyond testimony, which is discussed in the first half of this chapter, a forensic social worker may also speak at a client's sentencing hearing. When a defendant is sentenced, it is customary for the judge to allow the defendant to make a statement, friends or family to speak on behalf of the defendant, and professionals to speak about the defendant. Often, a forensic social worker may submit a written report for sentencing but also choose to speak at the defendant's sentencing hearing as well. A forensic social worker may choose to speak to the judge directly about a myriad of topics, such as the defendant's childhood, including risk and protective factors; motivation for change and work the defendant has done since being arrested; and/or the appropriate sentence for the defendant based on treatment needs and other criminogenic factors.

While it is generally uncommon for the social worker to write a report and speak in court about the same issues, a forensic social worker and attorney may choose to have the forensic social worker speak at the sentencing for strategic reasons. The lawyer may be concerned that written information will not be read thoroughly or have the same impact as an oral presentation. The lawyer may also want to withhold information about the client from the district attorneys beforehand, as they may use that information to argue against the sentence that the social worker has recommended.

From a strengths-based perspective, which is a cornerstone of social work values and ethics, it can be really beneficial for the defendant to hear the social worker speaking about him or her at sentencing. Often, a forensic social worker may not be able to make an impact on the outcome of the case but can make a positive difference in the life of the defendant which is equally important and in line with the ethics and values of a social worker.

Pictures as Visual Aids

Photographs can be one of the most powerful visual aids that social workers have access to in their arsenal of work product tools. The adage "a picture is worth a thousand words" is entirely accurate when it comes to thoughtful and powerful representation of clients and their life histories. Pictures grab the attention of the audience in ways that a page full of black and white letters cannot. Photographs of clients as children with their families can humanize them and remind the audience member what they looked like (age, height, build) when they were experiencing exceptionally adverse life experiences like physical or sexual abuse. Forensic social workers often insert pictures into their biopsychosocial or mitigation reports to evoke emotion and perhaps nostalgia related to childhood in general which will carry over into empathy and greater understanding of the client's specific life history.

Particular photographs can also highlight mitigation themes or narratives like a dirty home, a black eye or other bruise on a small child, gang or drug paraphernalia, etc. On the other hand, photographs can also show protective factors like a positive adult role model, the one positive foster home in a client's long list of abusive or subpar foster homes, or the client playing team sports.

Additionally, photographs of clients in the present can be extremely powerful tools to demonstrate change in a client's behavior. Many individuals, who were sentenced to life without the possibility of parole as juveniles, are now adults and have matured and made concerted efforts to change their thinking and behaviors. Many are involved in events at their prison like dog training and fund-raisers for community causes. There may be photographs of the client with a dog he or she trained or at a fund-raising event. Many have completed their GEDs and some have even graduated college or received a master's degree. A picture of a client in his or her cap and gown in spite of not because of their circumstances is incredibly powerful. Many incarcerated clients also have family days with their loved ones and the pictures taken at their visits can visually show the support that the client will have, if and when he or she is released from prison.

Film as Work Product

Across the country, it is becoming more common to utilize short films to tell a client's story. While the defense team generally hires a videographer or other trained professional to capture video of the client and other mitigation witnesses talking on film, a social worker can be very involved in the planning, interviewing, and editing processes. A mitigation film is basically a mitigation report that has come to life. It should briefly tell the client's life history while focusing mostly on the risk factors that led the client to engage in unlawful behavior. The goal of a film is to humanize the client and make others feel more compassion and empathy for his or her life experience. A social worker can help this process by creating the film outline which is often very similar to the outline of a mitigation report. A social worker should also be present and help interview with mitigation witnesses on film. Ideally, the forensic social worker will have already interviewed several mitigation witnesses, then assist the videographer and attorney in selecting the mitigation witnesses that best corroborate the life-history narrative. The filmmaker, who has a strong understanding of the client's life story based on reviewing the social worker's biopsychosocial or mitigation report and speaking with the social worker at length, will then create a short film, utilizing the film outline but also allowing for creativity and flexibility in the client's narrative. The forensic social worker should also view the film during the editing phase to ensure that the client's life history is chronological and that the filmmaker is accurately portraying the client and the mitigation narrative.

Film has proven to be a valuable tool in advocating for more appropriate sentences for clients with district attorneys and at resentencing hearings with judges. A barrier to film becoming a more common way of telling a client's story is often the cost associated with creating the film from the equipment to the filmmaker's time to both film and edit. Many agencies across the country have come to value film as a powerful mitigation tool but others are still inhibited by said barriers. As technology improves and continues to become more user-friendly including video quality on cell phones and video editing applications, it is likely that short film will become an accessible mitigation tool for many.

Conclusion

The telling of a client's story is one of the most important and rewarding aspects of a forensic social worker's role on the criminal defense team. A social worker utilizes his or her training and skill sets to provide work product that tells the forgotten story of how a young child was set up to fail through neglect and maltreatment in childhood or conversely how a criminal charge is truly only a bump in the road for someone based on their protective factors and criminogenic needs. Work product can be used for the defense team during negotiations with the district attorneys and for the Court at sentencing. It ranges from opinion-based work product, including client interview notes and reports, to complex, fact-based work product that retells parts of a client's life history for the Court. A forensic social worker can also produce demonstrative materials that help to re-create aspects of a client's life history or future upon reentry by utilizing visuals that humanize and educate. Forensic social workers have the opportunity to change how the district attorneys and judge see the defendant through thoughtful creation of work product that seeks to provide understanding about an individual's life experiences and the interconnectedness of someone's past, present, and future. Most importantly, forensic social workers have the ability to help clients change how they see themselves through skill building, reframing their life-history experiences, and encouraging them to envision their futures differently. However, because work product can be so valuable to a client and his or her case, it is imperative that forensic social workers understand the rules of confidentiality and privilege as well as the limitations of both, depending on the state and kind of case in which the social worker is working, or it may limit its effectiveness.

References

A. v. District Court, 550 P.2d 315, 325 (Colo. 1976).

Borrell-Carrio, F., Suchman, A.L., & Epstein, R.M. (2004). The biopyschosocial model 25 years later: Principles, practice, and scientific inquiry. *Annals of Family Medicine*, *2*(6), 576–582.

Colorado Crim.P. Rule 16(1)(e)(1).

Engel, G. (1977). The need for a new medical model: A challenge for biomedicine. *American Association for the advancement of science, 196*(4286), 129–136.

Hartman, A. (1979). *Finding families: An ecological approach to family assessment in adoption.* Beverly Hills, CA: Sage Publications.

Hartman, A., & Laird, J. (1983). *Family-centered social work practice.* New York, NY: The Free Press.

Hawkins, J.D., Catalano, R.F., & Miller, J.Y. (1992). Risk and protective factors for alcohol and other drug problems in adolescence and early adulthood. *Psychological Bulletin,* 112, 64–105. Cited in the figure 6.4.

Kagle, J. (1995). *Social work records* (2nd ed.). Long Grove, IL: Waveland Press.

Luepker, E., & Norton, L. (2002). *Record keeping in psychotherapy and counseling: Protecting confidentiality and the professional relationship.* New York, NY: Brunner-Routledge.

McGoldrick, M., & Gerson, R. (1985). *Genograms in family assessment.* New York, NY: Norton.

People v. Martinez, 970 P.2d 469, 475 (Colo. 1998).

Prinstein, M., Boergers, J., & Spirito, A. (2001). Adolescents' and their friends' health-risk behavior: Factors that alter or add to peer influence. *Journal of Pediatric Psychology,* 26(5), 287–298. Cited in the figure 6.4.

Prison Rape Elimination Act. (2003). *Juvenile Facility Standards.* Retrieved from https://www.prearesourcecenter.org/sites/default/files/content/preafinalstandardstype-juveniles.pdf

Reamer, F. (2003). *Social work malpractice and liability: Strategies for prevention* (2nd ed.). New York, NY: Columbia University Press.

Reamer, F. (2005). Documentation in social work: Evolving ethical and risk-management Standards. *National Association of Social Workers, 50* (4), 325–335.

Rule 1.6, Confidentiality of information. (2013). In American Bar Association, Center for Professional Responsibility. Model rules of professional conduct. Retrieved from http://www.americanbar.org/groups/professional_responsiblity/publications/model_rules_of_professional_conduct/rule_1_6_confidentiality_of_information.html

Rule 5.3, Responsibilities Regarding non-lawyer Assistance. (2013). In American Bar Association, Center for Professional Responsibility. Model rules of professional conduct. Retrieved from https://www.americanbar.org/groups/professional_responsibility/publications/model_rules_of_professional_conduct/rule_5_3_responsibilities_regarding_nonlawyer_assistant.html

Slater, L.K., & Finck, K.R. (2012). *Social work practice and the law.* New York, NY: Springer Publishing Company.

7

FORENSIC SOCIAL WORK AND COLLABORATION WITH EXPERT WITNESSES

Hillary Vervalin, Ashley Ratliff, and Kathleen McGuire

Abstract

This chapter will provide an overview of the collaborative process of consulting with an outside professional on a defense team. In the legal realm, outside professionals are often referred to as "expert witnesses" and for purposes of this chapter, the legal term, "expert witness" or "expert," will be employed. Legal and evidentiary guidelines related to the admissibility of testimony and disclosure requirements of an expert will be discussed together with highlighting of a handful of outside professionals commonly retained by defense counsel toward the best representation of their client's interests, including forensic psychologists, clinical psychologists, neuropsychologists, and victim outreach specialists (VOS). Additionally, practical suggestions and case examples to best foster the collaborative efforts between the defense team and the expert will be described. These include how a forensic social worker can both collaborate with an expert toward a comprehensive understanding of the client while supporting and advocating for the client as they engage in the process.

Learning Objectives

- Recognize why experts are necessary and utilized on many defense teams
- Understand the considerations for a defense team before and during the process of hiring or consulting with an expert
- Grasp a better understanding of a few experts with whom social workers frequently work
- Identify types of expert work product
- Understand how the forensic social worker and the expert work together for the best outcome for the client

A client's legal case often has a myriad of issues that require support and consultation with professionals who are qualified to provide expertise on a particular subject. There are a variety of professionals who can speak to different factual issues within in a criminal case which may aid in the defense of the case. These include gun powder residue, fingerprints, or the trajectory of a bullet from a gun. While these kinds of experts are necessary and important to a client's defense, this chapter will focus primarily on professionals who can help the legal team understand issues which typically involve a social worker including the psychological or sociological functioning of a client, including his or her mental state, maturity or immaturity, IQ and/or cognitive functioning, diagnosis of a mental health disorder, immediate or long-term impacts of trauma, gang involvement in teenage years, among many others. These professionals are often referred to in the legal community as "expert witnesses" because their specialized knowledge allows them to testify about matters that others would not be allowed to testify.

The Use of Experts on Defense Teams

Each client's case is unique and offers a variety of issues, subject matter, or problem areas which impact the client's involvement in or culpability related to an alleged offense, the capacity of the prosecution to prove the case beyond a reasonable doubt, or to help explain to decision-makers (such as the prosecutor, judge, or jury) how a client came to be in the circumstances within which they find themselves. Attorneys are not experts in all fields or subject matter but are trained to identify the varying issues that impact a particular client's legal case. Similarly, forensic social workers are not experts in all fields either, but certainly have knowledge and skills many attorneys lack and can play an important role in helping to identify specific issues impacting a case, locate particular professionals with the necessary expertise, and collaborate or assist the particular expert with their evaluation and analysis of a client's case.

For instance, the evidence against a client may be fingerprint evidence, and an attorney may employ its own expert in this field to help distinguish or corroborate this evidence. Or, a client may have confessed to committing a particular crime, but the reliability of this confession is an issue and the attorney employs an expert in this particular field to assist the legal team in understanding these issues. A lawyer will likely locate and collaborate with an expert on these sorts of fact-based issues without the aid of a social worker. On the other hand, the defense-based social worker is often involved in helping to identify issues related to mitigation themes and a client's psychological or sociological functioning and helping the defense team develop and work with experts in these particular areas.

The purpose of an expert in a criminal case is to provide a more thorough and complete understanding of any given subject about which the professional may have increased knowledge, and of which the average person would not necessarily be aware. Often, the information is presented in terms of an opinion. In a trial, witnesses who lack specialized knowledge or experience are prohibited from offering opinions of such Federal Rules of Evidence. Most witnesses in a trial are simply testifying to their actual knowledge, perceptions, or observations about a particular fact. These witnesses are often referred to in the legal realm as fact or lay witnesses. Mental health professionals may fall into either category depending upon the type of testimony they intend to provide (Gordon, 2016). A lay or fact witness, can, for instance, testify that they observed a person drive through a red light, and further observed the car to be weaving across multiple lanes of traffic. This witness, however, would likely be prohibited from testifying that he believed the driver to be impaired by alcohol because this is an opinion that would require specialized knowledge or experience in order to be admissible evidence. If, however, the witness happens to be a police officer who has observed hundreds of individuals driving while impaired by alcohol, it is possible the witness could be qualified as an expert by the judge and allowed to testify to this opinion. This expert, or opinion, testimony is generally provided in order to assist whoever the decision-maker may be—likely the prosecutor, judge, or jury, depending on the particular case—to more completely understand the client's legal case or individual circumstances. A defense team that has already employed the use of a social worker is likely seeking to discover and clarify mitigation themes and information about the person's psychological and/or sociological functioning, and these themes may require additional expert consultation.

Whether a professional will be qualified as an expert and allowed to testify as such is governed by the rules and laws in the particular jurisdiction in which a case is pending. An attorney is required to have sufficient knowledge and understanding of these specific rules and laws. In court, the judge will make this determination based upon the governing rules of evidence and case law (Fradella, Fogarty, & O'Niell, 2003). The attorney will also be the person who determines whether a specific professional will ultimately be qualified as an expert in the community. Generally, the qualifications necessary to be considered an expert in a legal sense will vary depending on the area of expertise and subject matter, and whether the specific professional has specialized knowledge, educational background, and/or experience to render an opinion on the particular certain subject matter.

The qualifications and expertise of a particular expert may also depend upon the ultimate use for the expert; in other words, who is the audience? In some cases, the attorney may determine that there is no benefit or legal basis to presenting expert testimony to a jury at trial, but the expert may be useful for persuading the prosecutor to dismiss charges, offer a fair resolution to the case, or persuade a judge to impose a more lenient sentence. The rules governing the admissibility of expert testimony at a trial are far more restrictive than those required by a judge outside of trial. Additionally, an expert known to be extremely persuasive to a jury may not be someone that the district attorney prosecuting the case finds compelling. Again, it is the attorney's duty in representing a client to know, understand, and make decisions with full consideration of these issues.

Considerations in Hiring or Consulting with an Expert

Collaboration with an expert who can assist in providing information about mitigation themes or the psychological and/or sociological issues impacting a client begins with identifying the right expert. This is a team effort, but the attorney will likely rely on the forensic social worker for input in this area.

One of the most important considerations of whether to consult or retain the sort of expert with whom a social worker would ordinarily collaborate relates to the impact of disclosure requirements. As discussed at length in Chapter 6, "Work Product" and in Chapter 2, "Guiding Principles of Practice," an attorney's work product and the work product of its agents and consultants, including that of expert witnesses employed by the defense, are considered confidential and not subject to disclosure requirements. In returning to the example of a fingerprint expert, it is quite possible that an expert would corroborate the prosecution's evidence and thereby implicate a client in the commission of a crime. Attorneys are advocates for their clients and should not have to be concerned about creating damaging evidence and working against their clients' best interests. It would certainly not be in a client's best interest to employ any sort of expert under any circumstance if an attorney was required to disclose incriminating information to the prosecutors. If this were the case, attorneys would be at an obvious disadvantage and not in a position to fully and adequately investigate the client's case. To promote effective representation, the use of this hypothetical fingerprint expert is generally protected as work product. Like many rules, though, this general work product protection is not absolute.

Depending upon how an expert is utilized, and the legal requirements in a particular state or jurisdiction, the work product of an expert, who is knowledgeable about the psychological or sociological issues impacting a client, may be subject to mandatory disclosure requirements whether or not that particular expert is ever called as a witness in a case. Attorneys are knowledgeable about these considerations and should advise, educate, and counsel the social worker when working with outside experts. However, consideration around the use and selection of appropriate experts requires at least a basic understanding of the legal rules around admissibility of the expert testimony and potential disclosure requirements.

It is often an extremely important and useful function of the forensic social worker to identify potential experts depending on the specific subject matter, and then vet the potential expert with colleagues and others who have experience with the subject matter or the expert. Once a specific expert is identified and vetted, the attorney, often with the forensic social worker's involvement, will meet with the expert to cover the basics of engagement, obtain an understanding of how the expert can potentially assist the client, and provide information to the expert about the particular issues involved in the case.

Experts Are not Defense Team Members—Disclosure Requirements and Work Product Considerations

As mentioned earlier, there are significant disclosure requirements when employing the use of an expert. Minimally, if an expert witness will testify at trial, it is highly likely that all information upon which the expert relied in formulating his/her opinion will likely be disclosed to opposing counsel. The reason for this is based on a fundamental concept of fairness. If a witness is going to testify to something that only someone with this expert's knowledge, skills, and expertise can comprehend, it is only fair for the other side to have full disclosure of all information the expert considered in reaching his or her conclusions. Therefore, thoughtful attention, before the expert is even retained, must be taken into consideration when hiring or contracting with a particular expert.

An expert witness may act in the role of consultant to the defense team. In this capacity, the expert will never be asked to testify or provide any sort of direct service to the client. An expert witness may also perform a review of records and offer opinions concerning various areas of subject matter contained within these records. In either of these cases, there is less risk of disclosure of confidential, personal, and potentially even incriminating information otherwise not subject to disclosure. Likely, the most common use of experts, though, in the area of psychological or sociological functioning involves utilizing an expert who will perform an evaluation of the client. And, it is this area which can often be fraught with risk of mandatory disclosure requirements, in large part because an evaluation, including the results, may require disclosure to opposing counsel. Disclosure is possible, even if the expert witness never testifies, and the results of the evaluation are not known prior to venturing into this area. The most common area illustrating this risk is when a client pleads Not Guilty by Reason of Insanity, often referred to by the acronym NGRI (which has various forms in most, but not all, states). In many jurisdictions, this plea alone will require a waiver of confidentiality to all mental health, psychological and psychiatric evaluations, and treatment of the client throughout the client's life. In some states, this sort of mandatory waiver of all privilege related to any prior mental health evaluation or treatment occurs in cases in which the prosecution is seeking the death penalty against the client and the defense chooses to call an expert at the sentencing trial. Engaging an expert to perform an evaluation of a client must necessarily involve a thorough discussion and consideration of this risk. The particular evaluation that the expert may perform should similarly involve this consideration. For instance, if a plea of NGRI is possible, and the defense has retained a psychologist for purposes of evaluation, the defense team may discuss with the expert whether or not personality testing is appropriate and consider all the various outcomes of any such testing, keeping the disclosure requirements at the forefront of the conversation.

As a reminder and discussed in Chapter 2, "Guiding Principles of Practice," criminal defense-based forensic social workers are members of the criminal defense team. This means that they work under the same umbrella of privilege and confidentiality as other team members including attorneys, investigators, and paralegals. The forensic social worker may have the same or even enhanced qualifications as an expert witness. However, there are often very good reasons to utilize an outside professional as the expert witness. Mandatory disclosure requirements are one such good reason. Other reasons include the enhanced credibility and lack of bias inherent in an expert witness who is not affiliated with the defense team other than the fact that the defense retained the expert. For example, a clinical child psychologist who has been practicing for many years in that particular field and administers various tests to a client to reach clinical conclusions and suggest interventions will likely hold more weight in court and with opposing counsel than the forensic social worker who is a member of the defense team and may have a vested interest in the client and the case outcome.

Examples of Various Experts Who Work with a Defense Team

The Forensic Social Worker as Expert Witness

A forensic social worker can certainly be qualified as an expert witness in most jurisdictions. However, if the defense team is considering engaging a forensic social worker as an expert, thought should be given to whether or not the forensic social worker should also be an active member of the defense team. As stated earlier, concerns related to confidentiality and the waiver of privilege, as well as perceived bias, would factor into this consideration.

The general professional requirements for most forensic social workers include an undergraduate degree, a master's degree in social work, and, often, licensure. To become a licensed clinical social worker, an individual must complete 3,360 hours of supervised work experience in the field of social work over at least 24 months and 96 hours of supervision (48 of which must be individual) with a licensed clinical social worker. It is likely that each social worker who works on a defense team has a diverse employment history related to social work, a variety of internship or field experiences, and varying areas of interest and familiarity.

Potential areas of expertise for a forensic social worker include childhood and adolescent development, risk and protective factors throughout a child's formative years, risks and impacts of substance use, the impact of head injuries on cognitive functioning and behavior, intellectual disabilities, trauma and trauma-informed care, fetal alcohol syndrome, attachment, cultural dynamics, among many other areas. Forensic social workers could be tasked with performing some type of developmental assessment because of their skills and training, whether they are acting as a member of the defense team or as an outside expert witness.

Forensic and Clinical Psychologists as Experts

Forensic psychology is considered a subspecialty of the field of psychology and involves the application of the professional's expertise to a legal setting. Clinical psychology is also a subfield of professional psychology that utilizes scientific knowledge to provide psychological assessment and intervention to patients (Gordon, 2016). In most cases, the clinical psychologist is diagnosing and treating a patient, whereas the forensic psychologist is most frequently performing an evaluation and formulating impressions and recommendations regarding a client to provide to someone involved in the legal system (Gordon, 2016).

Although many forensic psychologists are board certified in this specialized area, it is not necessarily a requirement for the expert to have this specialized certification. A clinician is certainly capable of performing an evaluation, which would subsequently be utilized in a legal setting. It is perhaps easiest to distinguish the clinical versus forensic psychologist by thinking that the clinician diagnoses and treats, while the forensic psychologist evaluates and recommends. Members of the defense team should know in advance the types of testing being administered by the expert practitioner, what these tests measure, what they mean and the potential ramifications. A conversation between the defense team and the hired expert should occur before the client is introduced to the expert.

Neuropsychologists as Experts

Neurology and neuropsychology are in the subspecialty of psychology that focus on the connection between the central nervous system, most notably the brain, and an individual's behavior (Clinical Neuropsychology, 2018; Gordon, 2016). A neuropsychologist will address a wide range of conditions related to the nervous system function, including dementia, Parkinson's disease, traumatic brain injury, seizure disorders, among many others. A neuropsychologist is tasked with interpreting the medical and scientific functions of the body in relation to a person's identity including their social history and culture (Clinical Neuropsychology, 2018).

A neuropsychologist can assist the defense team, and ultimately the decision-maker, better understand how a person processes information, uses and understands language, and the flexibility of their problem-solving and executive functions. Issues with problem-solving can impact the client's behavior and emotional management, especially in younger individuals (Steinberg, 2011), and be extremely helpful in determining the extent to which a client's behavior may have been affected by traumatic brain injury.

Let's take a closer look at Ben's case in the context of expert witnesses. Although there is very little documentation about Ben's history of head injuries, he self-reports and his family confirms that he has had at least two concussions—one from a car accident and the other from playing football. Moreover, Ben reports that he was "jumped into" the bloods gang at 14 and was beat up severely by other gang members. Ben lost consciousness during the attack and is unsure how many times he was hit and kicked in the head, but estimates that it was at least ten times. Ben and his parents report that he has experienced headaches, including migraines, memory loss, and trouble concentrating after he was "jumped in." After reviewing Ben's history and speaking with Ben and family members, it appears that all of his legal involvement began following his most severe head injury at 14 and his initiation into the gang. Although Ben did not go to the hospital after the attack, thus no medical records or diagnoses are available, he and his parents reported to the forensic social worker decreased concentration, memory loss, and personality changes including decreased empathy and increased aggressiveness. While the social worker is able to identify head injuries as a risk factor for Ben including symptoms and their impacts on his thinking and behavior, it is necessary for a neuropsychologist, who specializes in traumatic brain injuries, to evaluate Ben. As explained earlier, a neuropsychologist will have more experience and appear more credible to the court. Moreover, they are qualified to complete testing on Ben and opine about the condition of his brain in a way that a forensic social worker is not qualified to do. Ben's legal team will utilize the test results and recommendations for treatment from the neuropsychologist to advocate for Ben to remain in the community so that he can receive treatment for his traumatic brain injuries. Without the assessment and recommendations from the neuropsychologist, there would be no evidence of Ben's TBIs and changes in behavior aside from anecdotal confirmation from Ben and his family due to the lack of records available. Without the neuropsychologist, it would be much more difficult to argue for and secure a community sentence for Ben.

Victim Outreach Specialist

Defense-Initiated Victim Outreach (DIVO) is a program run out of The University of Texas at Austin by the School of Social Work and the Institute for Restorative Justice and Restorative Dialogue. Rooted in the tenets of restorative justice, the DIVO program was created after prosecution began on the Oklahoma City bombing case. The defense team wanted to contact the surviving victims and the families of those who lost loved ones (collectively known as victim survivors) to express profound and genuine sadness for what had occurred. Thus, DIVO was created by the nation's top experts in restorative justice and victim's crime services to help ease the tension between victims, their families, and the defense. A core belief of DIVO is that the victim survivors and a defendant(s) are connected by a tragic and life-altering experience. While this relationship is involuntary in many cases, at least initially, a victim's interaction with the defense through a trained and neutral VOS expert can help a defendant take responsibility and express remorse. Additionally, the process of interacting with and getting answers from the person who has brought irreparable harm can help the victim or his or her family through their healing process (Defense-Initiated Victim Outreach, n.d.; The Institute for Restorative Justice and Restorative Dialogue, 2009).

The VOS is contracted with by a defense team but works independently and neutral of the defense to communicate with victims of a particular crime. A VOS is an expert and does not have access to confidential and privileged defense team materials. According to the official manual, Defense-initiated Victim Outreach (DIVO): A Guide for Creating Defense-based Victim Outreach Services (2009), there is a step-by-step process for VOS services. These include:

1. After a referral for a VOS has been made, the defense team and the VOS meet in person to discuss expectations, the DIVO process, and to ensure that the selected VOS and requesting defense team are compatible.
2. Next, a VOS will draft a letter on behalf of the defense that introduces the DIVO process and the specific VOS and states when he or she will make contact. The letter also expresses condolence to the victim or family of the deceased victim and details any other victim survivors to whom the letter will be sent. Once the defense team and the VOS agree on the contents of the letter, the defense attorney sends the letter to the victim survivors on the attorney or law firm's letterhead.
3. After 4 or 5 days, the VOS sends his or her own letter to the same victim survivor(s). The VOS's letter includes much of the same information as the defense team's letter, including an expression of condolences, an explanation of the DIVO program and specifically why defense teams often utilize it, an example or two from other cases of what victim survivors have wanted or needed from the VOS, the choice of whether or not the victim

survivors would like to participate, an assurance of confidentiality if they choose to participate, a time line of when the VOS will follow up, contact information for the VOS, and an identical list to the defense team of other victim survivors who will receive the letter.

4. Within 3–4 days, the VOS follows up with a phone call to the victim survivor. It is recommended that the VOS only and leave voice mails a maximum of two times if he or she does not receive a response. The VOS must take no as a final answer. If the VOS does not hear back from the victim survivor, it is okay to try again after some months have passed but only if the victim survivor has not explicitly said no.
5. Once the victim survivor and the VOS make contact, the victim survivor is in control of how often they talk with the VOS, whether the meetings are over the phone or in-person, and what information they discuss. The information exchanged between the VOS and the victim survivor is always confidential. The VOS can only pass along information that the victim survivor has explicitly agreed to share with the defense. Additionally, the defense must agree to respond to every request that a victim survivor has even if the request cannot be completed.
6. After the initial contact, the interactions that take place between the VOS, the defense team, and the victim survivor(s) are organic, although the VOS will always follow the aforementioned rules. The relationship possibilities that can develop between a VOS and a victim survivor exist on a spectrum. In some cases, the DICO process yields a relationship between the victim survivor and the defense team or even the defendant. In other cases, the victim survivor(s) declines the VOS' offer and no further contact is made. Other times, the victim survivors get many questions answered by the defense team about the crime including motivations for and details of the crime, if they choose.

Detailed information about the philosophy and practices of the DIVO program can be found in the DIVO Master Manual linked in the reference section of this chapter. It should also be noted that while this chapter discusses expert work product including testimony, the VOS is not allowed to testify for the defense even under subpoena. Moreover, the VOS cannot produce any kind of written report for the defense regarding the individual DIVO process on that case. Both of these stipulations are agreed upon at the beginning of the DIVO process. According to the master manual, the prosecution could call a VOS to testify but that has not happened yet in any case.

Benefits of DIVO

If done correctly, DIVO can be beneficial for both the defense team including the defendant and the victim survivors and is unrelated to obtaining a better sentence or case outcome for the defendant. Rather, DIVO is beneficial because more often than not the "interests of the defense team and the victims are far from being mutually exclusive" (Branham & Burr, 2008, p. 1023). Victims want to tell their story and for the defendant to acknowledge and ultimately to validate their pain. Victims often have questions about the motivation for crime, details about the crime, and specifics about the defendant that only the defendant, through a VOS, can answer. Similarly, many defendants feel remorse that they wish to express to the victim survivors. The common interest of being acknowledged and heard makes victim-offender dialogue extremely valuable to both parties and a transformative part of the healing process for all involved.

DIVO can also be very beneficial on post-conviction and appeal cases. Often, physical time and emotional distance from the trauma of the crime can allow for dialogue to take place that would not have in a pre-trial case. Additionally, victim survivors often have less contact with the prosecution and prosecution-hired victim's advocates in post-conviction and appellate cases. Victim survivors might feel confused and have many questions and concerns, especially if those questions and concerns were not heard initially by the defense.

Selection of an Expert and Collaboration with the Defense Team

Identifying the Appropriate Expert

As discussed more thoroughly in Chapter 4, "Skills" it is imperative for the forensic social worker to identify risk and protective factors in the client's life so that he or she can begin to develop themes about trauma, systemic, institutional, and familial failures, physical and emotional disabilities, among many others, that may have contributed to an increased likelihood to engage in unlawful behavior (see Chapter 4 "Skills" for more on risk and protective factors). Through the process of mitigation investigation, including interviews with the client, family, treatment providers, and other mitigation witnesses, reviewing all available records on the client, and after uncovering risk factors that may have led the client to engage in unlawful behavior, the forensic social worker can help the attorney identify possible expert witnesses to evaluate the client, testify at an important hearing or provide an expert report that can be utilized throughout the legal process.

Important questions to consider when identifying appropriate experts include:

- What scope of knowledge will this expert provide?
- Will the expert meet the client or just opine about the client from information that the defense team has provided (often called a blind expert)?
- What kind of work product will the expert develop?

Expert Work Product

An expert witness may produce a variety of work product to assist the legal team or whomever will be utilizing the expert's results. This can range from basic summarization to very complex and in-depth efforts. Examples include an oral report of impressions and recommendations, a memorandum to provide a more concise review of information, a thorough evaluation containing all the information considered including comprehensive recommendations, charts and maps to depict significant areas of concern, and a power point presentation to illustrate more difficult concepts to a particular audience. The variety of work product produced by an expert is limited only by one's imagination, but what type and whether it is produced at all should be up to the attorney on the case rather than the expert. Other considerations include audience and setting, time frame that the expert has to evaluate and produce work product, expert strengths, the information the expert is conveying, among others.

If an expert creates a report, it should be reviewed to ensure it is factually accurate. Dates, details from records, family members' names, and the narrative of the client's life must all align with what the client, family interviews, records, and mitigation investigation by the forensic social worker have revealed. Accuracy is another reason for frequent contact between the defense team and the expert before, during, and after the expert's work on a case. The forensic social worker can help explain any family dynamics that exist that may inhibit the accuracy of information, including denial, poor memory, varying perceptions, mental illness, among other variables. Often times, a parent who is in denial about their child's history of sexual abuse may choose not to divulge those details to the social worker or expert. If the social worker, through records or client interviews, is aware that sexual abuse occurred but that the mother is in denial, he or she can preemptively relay that information to the expert which saves the expert additional time, effort, and/or confusion.

Aside from inaccuracies in factual information from the report, it is important to ensure that the expert fully understands the client and some of their mannerisms or characteristics which could be perceived negatively or inaccurately but are really just defense mechanisms or limited abilities to engage in ways an adult might expect. Recall Rodrigo, who came across as quiet and unwilling to provide detailed information about his life history, which might be interpreted as uncooperative. In his case, it would be important for the legal team to ensure that the expert is aware that Rodrigo grew up in the foster care system and has seen many professionals come in and out of his life; some that helped but many who did not. An expert can then consider whether he is truly being uncooperative or perhaps that he needs additional involvement by the forensic social worker whom he trusts before divulging personal information. Rodrigo's struggle to disclose personal information will be discussed more later.

Collaboration Between the Forensic Social Worker and the Client

As discussed in Chapter 4, "Skills" the forensic social worker builds rapport, and ultimately trust, with the client over time, which assists the legal team's efforts in advocating for the best outcome possible. The time and effort that the forensic social worker puts into understanding his or her client and the client's life history is invaluable to an expert who often does not have the time or resources to get to know the client like the social worker has done. The expert may only be able to meet with the client a limited number of times within a short period before opining about the client and the case. This can prove problematic for some clients who have difficulty trusting new people especially with personal and sensitive information.

Moreover, the social worker can complete a great deal of the groundwork in investigating and understanding the client's life history. As discussed in Chapters 4 and 6, "Skills" and "Work Product," of this book, one of the forensic social worker's most important roles is to develop the client's life history by reviewing all records from the client's past and, in many cases, completing a comprehensive biopsychosocial assessment that identifies and analyzes the risk and protective factors present over a client's childhood and adolescence. This information is crucial for an expert to review prior to evaluating the client (see Chapter 6, "Work Product" or a detailed explanation and example of a biopsychosocial assessment).

If we take a look at Rodrigo again, by the time he is 16 years old, he has already had numerous professionals come in and out of his life from caseworkers to clinical treatment professionals to Guardians Ad Litem (GAL). Rodrigo has been overwhelmed by professionals his entire life who promised to help him but, in his opinion, rarely follow through with what they have promised. This, coupled with Rodrigo's lack of faith in other adults in his life including his biological and foster parents, has caused him to severely distrust new professionals. In his current case, in which the district attorney's office is choosing to prosecute Rodrigo as an adult, has progressed, he has been introduced to two attorneys, one investigator, one criminal defense-based social worker, a new GAL, and a case manager at his juvenile facility, not to mention all of the professionals who work at the juvenile detention facility where he resides. It took the forensic social worker months to earn Rodrigo's trust by building rapport slowly and methodically. The social worker set weekly appointments with Rodrigo and did their best to keep them. Likewise, the forensic social worker did not delve into Rodrigo's history immediately. Rather, they spent at least three visits building rapport with him, including discussing hobbies and pastimes, favorite movies and music, etc. The social worker's efforts demonstrated to Rodrigo that they were invested in Rodrigo as a person, not just as a source of information. These forms of building rapport are easier for a social worker to achieve than an expert because the social worker sees Rodrigo frequently and is meant to have an ongoing relationship with him. This is not the expert's role and is often logistically impossible because of an expert's busy schedule that often includes full-time work in his or her own field of practice.

As exemplified earlier with Rodrigo, prior to the client and the expert's first meeting, a forensic social worker can utilize their rapport with the client to increase the client's trust in the expert or help the overall process run smoother. The forensic social worker can explain the value of the expert to the client so that the client has been informed by someone they trust. This may help the expert's interview with the client run smoother and yield better results because the client was mentally prepared for the interview process, felt comfortable, and knew what to expect. Additionally, before a client meets with an expert, the forensic social worker can help prepare the client for the interaction. If the client is prepared for the expert and knows information the expert has received from the defense team, it is likely that the client will be more open, relaxed, and trusting, which can yield more accurate and reliable results. If the client is apprehensive about meeting with the expert, the forensic social worker can support the client through an introductory meeting. If the client continues to struggle, it is possible for the forensic social worker to provide ongoing support to client. The forensic social worker can sit in on part of the meetings with the expert (with the consent of the expert and defense team) or be available to meet with the client directly after the expert meeting. A follow-up meeting directly after the expert meeting can be beneficial for the client as they can process and debrief any emotionally distressing or triggering information that was discussed. Additionally, and importantly, the forensic social worker can work with the client in between meetings with an expert, as the client may have been exposed to various traumas and reliving those memories through in-depth and intense meetings with an expert can cause re-traumatization and evoke uncomfortable or distressing feelings in the client. Evaluations by an expert can be painful and the forensic social worker can help the client understand and be prepared for the difficult feelings that may come up during or after an expert evaluation.

Finally, it is critical for either the attorney or the forensic social worker (perhaps together) to review any final reports or work product productions by the expert with the client. Just as the social worker reviews his or her biopsychosocial or other work product with the client, the legal team must review the expert work product with the client. Because most experts have very busy schedules and often travel for work or are not local to the client's state, it is unreasonable and often impossible for the expert to review the report with the client. Moreover, the social worker has already obtained all the information within the report previously in a slow, methodical, and client-centered manner which will likely make the client feel at ease in reviewing the expert work product and during the court proceeding. Likewise, reviewing expert work product with the client beforehand safeguard against possible inaccuracies and allows the client the opportunity to be fully involved in his or her defense. Additionally, if the case is likely proceeding to some sort of court hearing, the client will hear the opinions of the expert beforehand which can help them mentally prepare. The client should not be surprised or hear sensitive information that the expert will testify to for the first time at the hearing. It can be beneficial to prepare the client (and offer ongoing support) regarding the reviewing of expert work product and listening to testimony in court that can be re-traumatizing for clients.

The legal team on Rodrigo's case has decided that he should be evaluated by a forensic psychologist who can help contextualize how Rodrigo's early life experiences, including physical abuse, neglect and abandonment, and early system involvement have impacted his development. Rodrigo is unsure about the addition of this professional. He expresses frustration that he will have to talk about this life history again and sit through hours of testing. The social worker and attorney encouraged Rodrigo to be honest and reminded him that the legal team has already provided the expert with background information about Rodrigo that would be helpful to know. The information given to the psychologist included a biopsychosocial report from the social worker on the case, DHS records, school and IEP records, reports from the social worker of interviews with Rodrigo's mother, foster parents, and siblings. The social worker has explained to Rodrigo that when the psychologist visits with him, he or she will already have a great deal of knowledge about him. While this will not negate the expert's need to review certain parts of Rodrigo's life with him again, some which may be traumatic and difficult for him to discuss, it will minimize the need to review the unnecessary or irrelevant parts of Rodrigo's history. It will also allow the expert to quickly delve into issues that are relevant to the opinion that they will form.

Before Rodrigo meets with the psychologist, it is necessary for the social worker and attorney to meet or talk on the phone to discuss the goals of the evaluation and any pertinent information for the expert to know. Within this discussion, the social worker, who has spent many hours with Rodrigo, has noticed how Rodrigo is opening up more and does not seem as reluctant or unmotivated to share information as he did during the initial meetings with the social worker and the attorney. It may help the psychologist, who is only able to meet with Rodrigo one time, to explain that Rodrigo struggles to open up to new people, especially professionals, due to the quantity of people in and out of his life over the years. It will also be helpful for the social worker to explain how much time he or she has spent with Rodrigo and how long it took Rodrigo to open up to the social worker. The inclusion of the information about the social worker's time with Rodrigo not only adds credibility to the social worker's life-history information but also helps contextualize how Rodrigo may behave during the initial interview with the expert.

Collaboration Between the Forensic Social Workers and the Expert

Communication and ensuring the expert has access to all necessary information will maximize the use of an expert by a defense team. The forensic social worker is particularly well suited to work as a liaison with the legal team and expert, since the forensic social worker may have more familiarity and comfort with the subject matter of the expert, may have more client-specific information than other team members, and could potentially communicate quicker and easier with the client or family members. Collaboration with the expert can include very basic communication, including how many times the expert will see the client, to more intricate and complex details, such as directing the expert's attention to various pieces of collateral information. Each case will be unique and differ in what may be provided to the expert, and as explained earlier, thoughtful consideration must go into the material disclosed to the expert.

An expert should become involved in the case with ample time to review all materials from the defense team, which may include work product the social worker has created, such as time lines, genograms, biopsychosocial assessments, and reports from interviews with mitigation witnesses. Timewise, it may be unnecessary or impossible for the expert to review every document that exists regarding the client and their life. Thus, it can be beneficial for the expert to review work product that the forensic social worker creates and can aid the expert in understanding the individual nuances or intricacies of a case or client's circumstances (see Chapter 6, "Work Product" for specific examples). There may be legal issues to consider when providing materials to the expert that the attorney must discuss with both the forensic social worker and the expert prior to providing them to an outside independent expert. There may also be an inclination to withhold certain information because it presents the client in a negative light. However, any materials that the prosecution has provided, including discovery, should be disclosed to the expert, so the expert is not surprised at a hearing or trial in the future, even if the details do not portray the client in a positive manner. There also may be instances where the client may not want certain information shared with the expert. The attorney and forensic social worker can talk to the client about the information they do not want to disclose and why. The attorney can advise the client about why or why not some information should go to the expert. This is an example of how a strong sense of trust between the client and the team can prove beneficial. If the client trusts the forensic social worker and attorneys on their team and believes the team has the client's best interest in mind, they may be more likely to understand, and heed, the attorney's advice.

Next, it is extremely important that the defense team fully explores with the expert the scope of the evaluation, including what testing the expert will do, why certain tests may or may not be needed, and the scope of the expert's opinion on a given issue. It is equally important for the expert to explain what they believe to be the appropriate scope of their evaluation, based on the information the defense team has provided.

The expert can also benefit from discussing specific issues concerning the client with the forensic social worker because the social worker has come to understand the client well and can decode certain behaviors or thought patterns that may be unclear to the expert or inaccurately influence test results. Additionally, it is important for the forensic social worker to identify potential obstacles and triggers that may arise during the expert's evaluation process and to communicate those possibilities with the expert beforehand. Although it may be impossible to avoid triggers and feelings of distress when discussing uncomfortable topics, a social worker can speak to both the client and the expert regarding ways to minimize such problems as well as ways to handle such problems if or when they arise. If the social worker is worried that a client will become combative or silent after being triggered, it can be helpful to develop a safety plan with the client. It is also imperative that the expert is aware of possible triggers and the safety plan.

Additionally, the defense team and the expert should remain in contact and communicate frequently throughout the entirety of the evaluation process and while the expert is creating any work product. This can include in-person meetings, conference calls, and email. The expert should be updated on any new records or social history findings, or changes in the client's behavior, as it may impact his or her opinion.

As mentioned earlier, the defense team needs to provide relevant information to the expert about the client's life history, including a social history report if it exists, time lines, genograms, ecomaps, a review of records, and anything else that increases the expert's understanding of the client, his or her background, and the case. Although many experts will rely heavily on the information from the defense team, there are some experts who prefer interviewing important mitigation witnesses on their own. The social worker can help the expert identify these witnesses, connect important people with the expert, and even schedule interviews. Since the forensic social worker has likely built rapport with many of the family and mitigation witnesses, he or she can help the process of facilitating engagement between the expert and these individuals.

Practical Tips

- Communicate frequently with the attorneys and the expert on the case throughout the entirety of the expert's involvement
- Build rapport and trust with the client and their family which, in turn, will help facilitate communication and involvement with the expert
- Remain client-centered. Advocate for the client with the expert and support the client before, during, and after the expert's evaluation process
- Create work product with the expert in mind to help summarize, clarify, or draw attention to important themes
- Don't be afraid to point out information about the client, case, or relevant research. While the expert has specialized knowledge and experience, it is still a collaborative effort and the forensic social worker remains in the best position to inform the expert about the client
- Develop a working relationship with well-respected experts in different fields of study and practice as it will improve team dynamics and make the process run smoother

Conclusion

An expert plays a very important role on the legal team. The expert has specific knowledge that can inform the legal team, the district attorneys, and the Court. It is the legal team's responsibility to select an expert who has a positive reputation in his or her field and the legal community, and who will perform the expert services for the client and legal team in an individualized way. While there are several kinds of experts who can provide opinions for legal teams, social workers often coordinate and collaborate with psychologist, neuropsychologists, and VOS. Forensic social workers can improve the collaborative process by completing much of the groundwork for the expert by obtaining the client's life history, including record review, client interviews, and family interviews. The forensic social worker can also help the client understand the purpose of the expert's participation on his or her case and support the client through the process of working with the expert. Ultimately, the expert will provide work product that can help inform district attorneys, juries, or judges about the client and ideally provide a fair, appropriate, and more personalized outcome.

References

Branham, M., & Burr, R. (2008). Understanding defense-initiated victim outreach and why it is essential in defending a capital client. *Hofstra Law Review, 36*(3), 14th ser., 1019–1033. Retrieved April 4, 2018.

Clinical Neuropsychology. (2018). Retrieved February 29, 2018 from http://www.apa.org/ed/graduate/specialize/neuro.aspx

Defense-Initiated Victim Outreach. (n.d.). Retrieved March 1, 2018 from https://divo.irjrd.org

Federal Rules of Evidence 701 & 702.

Fradella, H.F., Fogarty, A., & O'Niell, L. (2003). *The impact of Daubert on the admissibility of behavioral science testimony.* 30 Pepp. L. Rev. 403 (April 2003).

Gordon, S. (2016). *Crossing the line: Daubert, dual roles, and the admissibility of forensic mental health testimony.* 37 Cardozo L. Rev. 1345 (April 2016).

The Institute for Restorative Justice and Restorative Dialogue. (2009). *Defense-initiated victim outreach master manual.* Retrieved March 9, 2018 from https://divo.irjrd.org/files/2016/04/master-manual.pdf

Steinberg, L. (2011). *Adolescence.* New York, NY: McGraw-Hill Institute.

8

SELF-CARE

Maren Willins and Ashley Ratliff

Abstract

This chapter will define self-care and explore its importance in the context of secondary traumatic stress. Social work as a profession can increase the risk of experiencing work-related stress. The following will define the various responses to stress and how the forensic social worker can prevent, identify, and cope through methods of self-care.

Learning Objectives

- Define and identify the terms associated with traumatic stress
- Identify the physical, emotional, mental, and behavioral responses to stress
- Identify various forms of physical, psychological, emotional, and spiritual self-care.

Social work as a profession and specifically forensic social work engages professionals into the deepest and often darkest parts of our clients' lives and, in turn, some of the most vulnerable places in society. In the role of a forensic social worker, we are trauma diggers. In this capacity, we read, listen, see, watch, and observe many stories—some of which we cannot unsee or un-hear, but rather, we dig even deeper to find meaning behind our clients' behaviors and provide options for consideration to the defense teams we work with and to those making important decisions about what will happen to our clients—state prosecutors and judges. To do the best work, we can as professionals, be fully there for our clients, we must understand how what we learn each day about our clients and then how we process that information toward best presentation toward the most beneficial outcome for our individual clients, impacts our personhood.

Definition of Important Terms

Social workers focus on taking care of others. An important part of being an effective social worker while also preserving longevity is a term called self-care. What exactly is self-care? Self-care is an activity you do which helps you maintain your physical, mental, or emotional health (NASW, n.d.). Some define self-care in social work as the "overlooked core competency…" (Jackson, 2014). We teach our clients the value of self-care and are equally able to benefit from our own self-care. "The need to engage in self-care is so great and the consequences so dire that the profession is stepping up in a variety of ways to deliver resources, provide training, and underscore the message that self-care is both fundamental and indispensable" (Jackson, 2014).

This chapter will define several important terms and provide suggestions for incorporating self-care practices daily, weekly, monthly, and yearly. By understanding the definitions and terms for various impacts of traumatic stress, we can begin to identify stress within ourselves. One cannot attend to his/her own self-care without first recognizing the signs of stress and transition in your life. Signs and symptoms of stress may be apparent in our physical, emotional, mental, and/or behavioral responses (Bensinger, DuPont & Associates, n.d.).

- Secondary traumatic stress—presence of post-traumatic stress disorder (PTSD) symptoms resulting from indirect exposure to traumatic material (NASW, n.d.)
- Compassion fatigue—term used interchangeably with secondary traumatic stress and burnout (NASW, n.d.)
- Burnout—emotional exhaustion and feelings of ineffectiveness due to work-related stress (NASW, n.d.)
- Vicarious trauma—a change in one's inner experience due to empathetic engagement with a traumatized person (NASW, n.d.)
- Compassion satisfaction—positive feelings deriving from competent performance as a trauma professional, characterized by positive relationships with colleagues and the conviction that one's work makes a meaningful contribution (NASW, n.d.).

Identifying Stress

Physical Responses: Change in sleep patterns, change in appetite, shallow rapid breathing, dizziness, headaches, muscle tension, increased heart rate, stomach upset.

Emotional Responses: Shock or numbness, anger toward others involved, fear, depression, guilt, frustration, sadness, feeling unsafe or vulnerable, loneliness.

Mental Responses: Confusion, difficulty concentrating, difficulty remembering details of event.

Behavioral Responses: Withdrawal from others, angry outbursts, crying, irritability, decreased energy/ambition, marital/relationship conflict, increased use of alcohol or medications, fear of being alone.

As many have stated and agree, social work is a high-stress profession. Practicing appropriate self-care is not only good role modeling but also imperative to maintain longevity in our careers, avoid burnout, and remain healthy. We cannot be present and healing for our clients and families if we are not for ourselves. Many social work jobs are within an agency where there are other social workers to support you in self-care, while other social workers operate more independently in the field or may be surrounded by professionals other than social workers.

Working as a criminal defense-based forensic social worker can be more isolating than other more traditional social work positions. Depending upon the setting, a lot of time may spent traveling alone—often times to remote areas to visit clients at facilities, jails, or prisons. There may be no central office and the forensic social worker operates as an independent member of a larger defense team comprised of other independent professionals working for one client or multiple clients. As a forensic social worker on a criminal defense team, a great deal of time is spent with clients one-on-one and more likely, within a correctional facility. Because of this isolation, appropriate self-care for the forensic social worker can be even more challenging and increases in importance. Additionally, criminal defense-based soçial workers are often working among legal professionals instead of a clinical organization of their social work peers. The personal dynamics among the various professionals (legal, correctional officers, other therapeutic professionals, academic professionals, government workers) can also affect the social worker just as much as the emotions involved in supporting our clients.

Additionally, much of the client populations served by forensic social workers are members of special populations, often living in low socioeconomic communities, and experience increased negative involvement in the legal systems. Many individuals within our client population are dealing with mental health issues, substance abuse, developmental delays, and/or a lack of effective services and resources. Taken altogether, this can take a significant toll on the forensic social worker. Due to the potential isolation, professional dynamics and emotional impact of this work, a specialized self-care plan and a connection to other forensic social workers are strongly encouraged.

Discussion

As forensic social workers in this role, we will have a variety of cases with unique clients who have experienced varying forms of life experiences including a great deal of trauma. When managing a caseload as trauma diggers, it is critical to weave in a self-care plan during busy times as much as times when the work flow is much lower. Imagine carrying a caseload of Rodrigo, Ben, Deb, and Jaime with various mitigation trips out of your home state during the course of a short period of time with critical hearings in between. These are the stories that you cannot un-hear that you need to process in order to best assist the defense team in securing the best legal outcome. Mitigation development is crucial in any case, and witnessing these events through interviewing family, friends, and other relatives weighs upon our minds, whether we are conscious of this or not.

Imagine you are working on Deb's case: *In order to develop the critical mitigation themes in Deb's case, the team takes a mitigation trip to Detroit, Michigan, to see if some of Deb and her mother's family members can be located and to make an effort to track down various childhood records, including records from school, medical institutions or doctors, and the Department of Human Services (DHS). DHS became involved in Deb's life when allegations of sexual abuse were reported about Deb's mother's boyfriend. Lastly, records need to be obtained from the Arc agency that has provided services to Deb since about the age of 8. Financial constraints within your agency dictate that only 3 days are allotted for this trip. As soon as you arrive in Detroit, you and the criminal defense investigator have mapped out a plan of possible home addresses for relatives together with the different agencies that may have records. Because Deb is now 30 years old, some of these childhood records may not be available or perhaps may have been destroyed after so much time. The neighborhood where Deb's family resided when she was young and where you finally find one aunt, is one of the poorest neighborhoods around Detroit. You have stopped by two possible houses for Aunt Mae (Deb's maternal aunt)—one was a vacant lot within a series of disheveled-looking, single-family homes, and the second attempt brought you and your investigator to a boarded-up house which had bullet holes around the front windowsills. Finally, you make a third attempt to find Mae and she is home. Mae reluctantly invites you and your investigator into the small house. You and your investigator are both white and your appearance on Mae's doorstop seem to be slightly unsettling. After introducing yourself as Deb's team working to help her, Mae, who always had a loving bond with Deb, agrees to sit down with you to talk about her and the family. The stories that unfold are filled with generational abuse, sexual abuse allegations and you learn that Deb's mother has consistently placed Deb with caregivers who abused her or left her to fend for herself since a very young age. You realize that there is so much more to Deb's story than anyone ever imagined from brief reviews of records and from the miscellaneous information Deb has been able to provide over time building rapport with her. Mae provides a great deal of information about other family members whom you are able to track down while in Detroit, which piles on further stories of trauma, abuse, and suffering that Deb experienced as a young child. In the midst of these interviews, you have come to learn a great deal about gathering records from multiple state agencies across the Detroit area—some agencies have hostilely told you records from that long ago have been destroyed. When you ask for a letter of confirmation for that, finally at the Detroit*

Department of Human Services, a huge box of records and files is produced for you and your investigator to look through. Although many more days could be spent in Detroit to uncover details of Deb's early years, you have to leave to put these pieces together and also move on toward another mitigation trip quickly approaching.

After three intense days visiting with Deb's relatives in Detroit, you are tasked with mitigation interviews in Rodrigo's case, which has you deep in the impoverished rural community where he grew up. You have a Spanish-speaking investigator with you to assist in these interviews; however, the language barrier does make these interviews much more complicated. Rodrigo has a large family in the hills of rural Mexico and you spend 4 days interviewing about 10 people. Rodrigo's family in Mexico is warm, loving, and very supportive to Rodrigo. They all want to help him however they possibly can, which is shared with you via an interpreter and these interviews all take several hours at a time. After the trip to Mexico, you must put together a biopsychosocial assessment with the information provided by family from both Mexico and locally—there are different versions of some events of Rodrigo's life which go toward some of the mitigation themes of the case. Additionally, you are working under a tight time line, with only months to prepare for the reverse-transfer hearing, working with experts who will meet with Rodrigo one to two times, and you will be tasked with reviewing much of the material that is to be presented at the hearing to Rodrigo ahead of the hearing so that he can process the information before hearing it for the first time in open court.

How do you unwind from these trips? How can a forensic social worker incorporate self-care into a packed schedule filled with travel to meet with witnesses in the trauma digging efforts? What are some strategies to incorporate between travel for these cases and important hearings that may be filled with intense information presented in Court from your mitigation development?

Forms of Self-Care

Appropriate self-care can help to prevent symptoms of stress and combat these responses to stress. There are various forms of appropriate self-care that include connecting with other forensic social workers, exercise, happy hour, journaling, therapy, support from family and friends, maintaining a central office, utilizing supervision, healthy eating, and more. There are also inappropriate and unhealthy habits and behaviors that can occur when one is not attending to their own needs in this forensic social work field. Excessive stress may manifest itself into excessive substance use, the development of vicarious trauma, relationship issues, and/or burnout. Appropriate methods of self-care may include (Bensinger & DuPont, n.d.; Cox & Steiner 2013):

Physical Self-Care

- Eat regularly
- Eat healthily

- Exercise
- Get regular medical care for prevention
- Get regular medical care when needed
- Take time off when sick
- Get massages
- Fun physical activity (dance, swim, walk, run, play sports, sing)
- Get enough sleep
- Wear clothes you like
- Take day trips or vacations
- Make time away from phones/computers (including your personal cell phone)
- Fill in: ________________________________

Psychological Self-Care

- Make time for self-reflection
- Psychotherapy
- Journal
- Read (literature unrelated to work)
- Do something at which I'm not the expert or in charge
- Notice my inner experiences (listen to my thoughts, judgments, beliefs, attitudes, feelings)
- Engage my intelligence in a new area
- Practice receiving from others
- Say no to extra responsibilities sometimes
- Ask for help when needed
- Fill in:________________________________

Emotional Self-Care

- Spend time with others whose company I enjoy
- Stay in contact with important people of my life
- Give myself affirmations
- Find ways to increase my sense of self-esteem
- Re-read favorite books
- Review favorite movies
- Identify comforting activities, objects, people, relationships, places, and seek them out
- Allow myself to cry
- Find things to make me laugh
- Express my outrage in social action, letters, donations, marches, protests
- Play with my kids/dogs/animals
- Garden
- Fill in: ________________________________

Spiritual Self-Care

- Make time for reflection
- Spend time with nature
- Find a spiritual connection of community
- Be open to inspiration
- Be aware of nonmaterial aspects of life
- Try at times not to be in charge or expert
- Identify what is meaningful to me and notice its place in my life
- Meditate
- Pray
- Sing
- Have experiences of awe
- Fill in:____

Maintaining Good Self-Care

Self-care works best when practiced daily and weekly. Time must be blocked daily and weekly to attend to one's own self-care. A good way to maintain this is by making your own personal self-care plan individualized and a way of life (Cox & Steiner, 2013). Laura van Dernoot Lipsky with Connie Burk (2009) point out how "The more personal our connection to our work, the greater the gifts we bring to it-perhaps. At the same time, the more we identify with the type of trauma we're exposed to, the greater its impact on us may be" (19–20). Individualizing good self-care involves knowing what attracts you to this work. Is there a personal connection to this work or population? If so, have you taken the appropriate steps to protect yourself from the vulnerabilities associated with the work? "…if you are working with a population with whom you have a history, you may feel a rawness as you approach your work" (Lipsky, p. 20). These questions are critical to think about and analyze over time within the profession of forensic social work and within a criminal defense team; however, the work is structured (within and office or agency, or independently in the field).

Maintaining appropriate self-care is similar to investing in the stock market. It is important to diversify and invest both in the short term and in the long term. Additionally, self-care may involve taking risks. The long term may include a vacation every year, saving money for a new gadget, taking a week off from work, going to that concert in 2 months, and/or having a spa day with friends every quarter. Short-term self-care may include daily morning meditation, the 10 am latte, 30 minutes of exercise every other day, weekly chocolate cake, Friday night services, a Sunday hike, and/or Thursday happy hour with colleagues. At times, taking a risk may be the most rewarding form of self-care. This may include learning Portuguese (out of desire to learn a new language, not for work), taking an art class, brewing beer, taking a day trip to a new place (on the bus), and/or adopting a pet. Diversifying is a key component of maintaining individual self-care. Happy hour alone, while this may be part of a self-care plan, does not take care of spiritual, emotional, psychological, and physical care.

Obstacles to Self-Care

Unfortunately, there are many reasons social workers and other helping professionals forget or avoid their own self-care. Oftentimes, one of our biggest obstacles is ourselves. We need to get out of our own way! Start small and build from there over time. Valid obstacles revolve around time and money. Social workers, especially right out of graduate school, have student loans, busy work schedules, and possibly families to care for and be with. Some social workers do not participate in self-care because of "lack of energy, too many responsibilities, and fear of appearing weak or vulnerable" (Jackson, 2014). Luckily many forms of self-care require little to no money and time at all. Start with these, make and drink coffee/tea without distraction, take a walk, journal, sing, dance, do yoga stretches, pray, meditate, or read for fun. Encourage yourself to start with one or some of these for 10 minutes per day. Ignoring your self-care may lead to burnout, compassion fatigue, or vicarious trauma. Burnout is defined as "physical or mental collapse caused by overwork or stress" (Merriam-Webster). Burnout is commonly associated with social work jobs and many can become fatigued by his/her work. Self-care can prevent and remedy burnout in social work careers. Like burnout, compassion fatigue may also be prevented and remedied with self-care. Compassion fatigue is when a professional may "get a little jaded to caring" (Dr. Charles Jacob, April 20, 2017 webinar). For both burnout and compassion fatigue, it can be as simple as working a little less and getting a hobby.

Vicarious trauma is often referred to as the "cost of caring" (Figley). Dr. Charles Jacob describes vicarious trauma as "something about your worldview has changed… an overgeneralization of the horrors of the world to everything. Self-care isn't going to change your altered view of the world" (April 20, 2017 webinar). When vicarious trauma occurs, one should look toward a more meaningful intervention such as therapy, a sabbatical or possibly consideration of a career change.

Practical Tips

The key to an effective self-care plan is to make it individualize and frequent. In other words, make it work for you! The following is an example of my personal plan (Maren Willins):

- Daily = sleep hygiene, eat healthy, exercise
- Weekly = journal, happy hour, outdoor time

- Monthly = MNO (Mom's night out), date night, massage
- Yearly = vacation, family week.

Going back to being the forensic social worker on the criminal defense teams for the case study clients presented in this book and more. Consider including at least 1 hour of day time blocked for yourself and no other members of the team during mitigation trips where you can go for a walk, check out the hotel gym or even do a yoga session online; have a family member send you videos of your young children at home; get a 20-minute massage. Also build in space between the trips that is for personal time in addition to accomplishing other work. Calendar management is critical to this work and for ourselves.

Conclusion

The authors are challenging each reader to start today with a new (or revamping an old one) self-care plan. Challenge yourself to make your own plan including at least one component to address your spiritual, emotional, psychological, and physical self-care needs. Challenge yourself to do something for your own self-care on a daily/every other day, weekly, and monthly basis. Finally, reevaluate how your self-care plan is working. Are you sticking to your plan more days than not? Are you incorporating aspects of your plan no matter where you are or how busy the work gets? Is something or someone constantly being avoided? Perhaps cooking a healthy meal every night is more than what is feasible? Instead, try cooking a healthy meal three times per week. Perhaps happy hour is becoming a daily event. Perhaps limit it to once per week or replace some with tea. Just as you would reassess your client and his/her treatment plan; afford the same to your own care.

References

Bensinger, DuPont & Associates. (n.d.). www.bensingerdupont.com

Cox, K. & Steiner, S. (2013). *Self-care in social work – a guide for practitioners, supervisors, and administrators*. Washington, DC: NASW Press.

Figley, Charles (2002). Compassion fatigue: Psychotherapists' chronic lack of self care. *Journal of Clinical Psychology*, doi:10.1002/jclp.10090.

Jackson, Kate (2014). Social work self-care – the overlooked core competency, *Social Work Today, 14*(3), 14.

Lipsky, Laura Van Dernoot & Connie Burke (2009). *Trauma stewardship – an everyday guide to caring for self while caring for others*. San Francisco, CA: Berrett-Koehler Publishers.

National Association of Social Workers (NASW). (n.d.). (2018). www.sowialworkers.org

National Organization of Forensic Social Work (NOFSW). (n.d.). (2018). www.nofsw.org

INDEX

Page numbers in *italic* indicate a figure and page numbers in **bold** indicate a table on the corresponding page

For Product Safety Concerns and Information please contact our EU representative GPSR@taylorandfrancis.com
Taylor & Francis Verlag GmbH, Kaufingerstraße 24, 80331 München, Germany

www.ingramcontent.com/pod-product-compliance
Ingram Content Group UK Ltd.
Pitfield, Milton Keynes, MK11 3LW, UK
UKHW021502240926
475702UK00035B/147
* 9 7 8 1 1 3 8 2 2 1 5 3 6 *